Perspectives of Divorced Therapists

Through interviews with divorced therapists from diverse cultures, philosophies, and generations, this book explores how a therapist's divorce impacts their work with clients in couples therapy. Interviewees speak of their own experiences with trauma recovery, countertransference, self-disclosure, resilience, and other issues during and after divorce. These experiences are also correlated to previous studies exploring the counseling process and variables that might affect the outcome. Through the stories of other professionals, therapists will gain insight into developing self-awareness and utilizing the *person-of-the-therapist* model to successfully navigate the impact of their own life crisis as they work with clients. This text will provide enlightenment and courage for divorced or divorcing therapists, as well as any therapist who lives through the experience of managing their own relationship struggles while continuing to lean in and support their clients.

Tanya Radecker, PhD, LPC-S, NCC, RN, is an ICEEFT-certified EFT supervisor with a private practice in New Orleans, Louisiana. Additionally, she serves as the executive director of the Louisiana Community for Emotionally Focused Therapy. Dr. Radecker lectures at universities and conferences and provides educational workshops across the state for other clinicians learning EFT. She is also a certified clinical hypnotherapist who specializes in working with couples and individuals who deal with trauma, high conflict, and sexual assault/abuse.

This timely and innovative book helps transform the shame and stigma of divorce into a powerful instrument of empathy to reach deeper and connect more intimately to the most vulnerable parts of ourselves and our clients.

George Faller, LMFT, President of New York Center for Emotionally Focused Therapy, Director of Training at the Greenwich Center for Hope and Renewal

Dr. Radecker's compelling interviews, interwoven with her authentic self-of-the-therapist disclosure throughout this book, offer a unique glimpse into the emotional world of we human beings who are also psychotherapists. Revealing both the challenges and potential benefits to our work, it is of value for any psychotherapist going through a crisis in their own personal life.

Jodi Ames-Frankel, PhD, ICEEFT-certified EFT supervisor

In *Perspectives of Divorced Therapists*, Dr. Radecker addresses the dilemma that ALL therapists have. Is it possible to have personally experienced every presenting problem a client brings to the counseling room? And is it necessary for the therapist to have been 'successful' in grappling with each of those issues? The author candidly shares her personal story and includes the journeys of other clinicians in addressing those important questions.

Dee Adams, PhD, LPC, LMFT, couple's therapist in private practice for 30 years

Dr. Tanya Radecker is an accomplished counselor who also happens to be divorced. Based on her clinical experiences and her research, she has written this book that should be read by all divorced mental health professionals. In the book, Dr. Radecker leads divorced mental health professionals through the process of assessing their own thoughts and feelings about their own divorce in preparation for putting those issues aside as they help couples navigate their relationships. She also helps divorced mental health professionals decide whether to disclose they are divorced, a decision that must be made individually by each divorced mental health professional.

Theodore Remley, JD, PhD, Professor of Counseling, Booth-Bricker Endowed Professor, Department of Counseling and Behavioral Sciences, University of Holy Cross

PERSPECTIVES OF DIVORCED THERAPISTS
Can I Get it Right for Couples?

Tanya Radecker

NEW YORK AND LONDON

First published 2019
by Routledge
711 Third Avenue, New York, NY 10017

and by Routledge
2 Park Square, Milton Park, Abingdon, Oxon, OX14 4RN

Routledge is an imprint of the Taylor & Francis Group, an informa business

© 2019 Taylor & Francis

The right of Tanya Radecker to be identified as author of this work has been asserted by her in accordance with sections 77 and 78 of the Copyright, Designs and Patents Act 1988.

All rights reserved. No part of this book may be reprinted or reproduced or utilised in any form or by any electronic, mechanical, or other means, now known or hereafter invented, including photocopying and recording, or in any information storage or retrieval system, without permission in writing from the publishers.

Trademark notice: Product or corporate names may be trademarks or registered trademarks, and are used only for identification and explanation without intent to infringe.

Library of Congress Cataloging-in-Publication Data
A catalog record for this book has been requested

ISBN: 978-1-138-24046-9 (hbk)
ISBN: 978-1-138-24047-6 (pbk)
ISBN: 978-1-315-28365-4 (ebk)

Typeset in ITC Legacy Serif
by Apex CoVantage, LLC

TO MY FAMILY, FOR THEIR UNCONDITIONAL LOVE, PATIENCE, AND SUPPORT.

CONTENTS

Acknowledgments ix

Preface xi

Introduction 1

1 *"Being"* a Mental Health Professional 11

2 Our Stories 31

3 Exploring Previous Views of Divorce: Impact
   of Our *FOO* 47

4 Working on Self-Awareness and Recovery 57

5 Is My Own "Stuff" Getting in the Way? 71

6 Do I Have Wisdom to Share? Am I Credible? 81

7 To Tell or Not to Tell 91

8 Am I More Likely to Encourage Disconnection? 103

9 Moving Forward 113

References 127

Index 141

ACKNOWLEDGMENTS

As I reflect on the process of completing a dissertation and this book, I am eternally grateful for the loving support, prayers, and encouragement of my family: Michael, Ian, Jourdan, and Quinn Brown. Many times, they showed extreme patience and tolerance when I was feeling a *bit stressed* and needed their help in navigating technology or just lightening my daily load. They were consistently charitable with their time in assisting with proofreading and editing a work that I am certain did not really capture their interest or fit into their busy schedules.

I also want to thank my parents, Thomas Radecker and Earline Roppolo. For 57 years their confidence in me has been unwavering. They taught me that all goals are achievable through hard work, persistence, and faith. Throughout my life, my parents have truly been my cheerleaders in the countless projects I decided to tackle. I firmly believe that without their consistent support and prayers, my journey in life would have been quite different.

I am eternally grateful to the gracious clinicians who willingly shared their personal stories with me. The topic of this research is often painful to share and yet they were open and forthcoming in sharing any insight they have learned. It was their goal that the stories might help fellow colleagues heal and move forward as they face their own challenges from the life crisis of divorce. Ultimately, their sharing supports the *person-of-the-therapist* and promotes a successful counseling experience for both the therapist and client.

To my major professor, Dr. Matthew Morris, thank you for the many hours spent reading and re-reading the numerous edits and revisions of my work. Your guidance and thoughtful comments were invaluable in my learning experience. To the professors on my committee, Dr. Theodore Remley and Dr. Carolyn White, I express my sincere appreciation for your support as well as honest and kind feedback. I also wish to thank the entire faculty of the University of Holy Cross Counseling PhD Program for their commitment to providing a quality educational experience with the patience and flexibility needed to support the overall well-being of the students.

A special thank you to the many friends in my EFT Community. For the past 5 years their support and encouragement has been a lifeline for this "pursuer." As I moved into a new phase of my journey, they helped me to navigate this *new challenge* of self-exploration. In the words of my dear friend Dr. Patricia Aptaker, "How would we look at this from an EFT perspective?"

Above all, I daily give thanks to the Lord for giving me an amazing family, a rewarding career, and the opportunity to share this work with colleagues. It is my hope that this book will not only provide insight into working with clients, but shine a light on the *person-of-the-therapist* and our journeys as human beings.

PREFACE

This book is based on my dissertation, "The Experience of Divorced Mental Health Professionals Working with Couples." My professional journey brought me into the field of mental health counseling later in life. As a R.N. and later a Neonatal Nurse Practitioner, I had spent over a decade supporting families through periods of stress and grief while simultaneously providing medical care to their infants. Although I was trained as a Resolve Through Sharing Counselor, my overall role was very "task oriented" and my goal was to "fix the problem." So, the transition to becoming a mental health professional was quite the challenge. It was no longer my role to "fix a problem"; my new role was to guide a client through an exploration of their journey and struggles—to shore them up while they dig deep into those places we all want to avoid. I quickly realized that I would need to explore my own fears, anxieties, raw spots, and triggers in order to be effective with my clients.

Right from the beginning, choosing a dissertation topic became the subject of many class discussions. I initially had a very different idea for my research, one that did not require me to hold up a mirror. It was not until I was approached to write a book that I decided to focus on something that would be more meaningful and an exploration of me. And, in discussing the topic with colleagues, it was clear

xi

that I was not alone. I was actually surprised at the number of mental health professionals who, despite their own painful relationships, continue to have a passion and commitment to working with couples.

My journey has included many twists and turns that I am certain have influenced my approach to working with clients. Just as with all life events, I believe that my relationships have woven a fiber into *self-as-person;* all aspects have been noticed—the beginning, the middle and the end. I have been married and divorced to the same man twice. Both times the divorce was amiable; there was no battle of lawyers or trying *to win.* We continued to function as *a family* with family holidays and vacations still being the norm.

In examining the ease in which I shift from spouse to friend, I wonder if my experience has colored my own feelings and thoughts surrounding divorce, hence influencing the interventions and therapeutic relationships with my clients. I must consider how this shapes my work as a couples therapist. Am I more likely to encourage others to walk away and find their relief? In our roles as clinicians, we must identify our own biases and how that affects our work with clients.

As I listened to the stories of the participants in my research, it became apparent to me that experiencing the *life crisis* of divorce presented unique concerns for mental health professionals. At some level, I believe clients are aware that their therapist is a human being: a person at risk for all the human afflictions and crisis. However, if the client is looking for expert advice in order to be successful with a specific life challenge, does the client expect that the "expert" was able to successfully navigate that particular challenge? And, what feelings arise for the therapist surrounding their own unsuccessful attempt at navigating a relationship?

INTRODUCTION

Relevance of the Topic

The goal of all licensed mental health professionals is to provide genuine, non-judgmental, supportive, and effective counseling services (Eells, Lombart, Kendjelic, Turner & Lucas, 2005; Karekla, Lundgren & Forsyth, 2004; Lee & Nichols, 2010). Each of the academic training programs strives to educate and enlighten students to be professional and skilled in the counseling process. Simultaneously, those in charge of educating future therapists are also endowed with the task of encouraging the students to dig in and explore their own personal issues. The expectation is that the students will gain insight, awareness, and mastery of the skill of maintaining separation between personal and professional life. However, as humans, what happens when professionals find themselves inflicted by the same life crisis that infiltrates the lives of clients? Do we falter and get sidetracked in our own pain and struggle?

So, what is the experience of divorced mental health professionals who are working with couples in distress and why is it significant? I searched for the insight into this question through both self-reflection and interviews with divorced mental health professionals across the United States: professionals who are committed to working with couples in an effort to de-escalate, repair, and navigate relationships.

1

As therapists, we are trained to be neutral, a "tabula rasa." But are we so heavily influenced by our own experiences with the life crisis of divorce that it affects our approach and choice of interventions with couples? What insight can we share with clients if we were not able to successfully preserve our own relationship? Do we see ourselves as "wounded healers" and worry that others will doubt our abilities?

I explored these questions for myself and I reached out to other mental health professionals and invited them to open a space for their own self-exploration. Eight therapists from different backgrounds, philosophies, generations, and ethnicities share their insights and stories as to how this "phenomenon" has impacted both their personal and professional growth. This is a journey to discover the innermost thoughts and feelings of therapists—thoughts that might be hidden at the bottom of the iceberg, deep below the surface. Perhaps the insight will serve as a guidebook for other therapists who are negotiating their own relationship and professional dilemmas. Possibly, our experiences will give others the courage to hold up the mirror and examine painful wounds and scars that are subtly influencing their work with clients.

Clients seek counseling to find solutions and guidance to save their marriages and families. Do some clients feel that an expert in couples counseling should be able to successfully navigate their own relationships and therefore might not consider a divorced therapist to have credibility? The therapists themselves might also struggle with self-doubt. Some research has reported that divorced therapists do experience struggles with self-esteem and self-doubt as a result of their own failed relationships (Johansen, 1993; Pappas, 1989; Schlachet, 1996). Do these feelings have the potential to infiltrate the therapeutic relationship and, ultimately, the outcome of the therapy?

Approximately 40%–50% of first marriages end in divorce, with an increase to 60% of second marriages and 75% of third marriages (Doss et al., 2016; Lebow, Chambers, Christensen & Johnson, 2012). What does this mean for mental health professionals and their relationships? The American Counseling Association has over 56,000 members, the National Association of Social Workers reports having more than 132,000 members, and the American Psychological Association has more than 122,500 members; this means there are at least 310,500 therapists in the United States who potentially will provide therapy to families or couples. These numbers do not include the thousands more therapists who do not belong to professional organizations, who might also be providing therapy to families or couples.

Based on the statistics, the potential number of divorced mental health professionals working with couples in distress is significant (Doss et al., 2016). Gaining insight into the most effective method for management of this personal life event is vital to maintaining a healthy and successful therapeutic relationship and process. Examining this phenomenon by utilizing heuristic inquiry method offers the possibility of gaining understanding of both the themes and echelons to which the divorce experience influences the therapeutic relationship and outcome of counseling (Moustakas, 1990).

The research for my dissertation explored specific questions surrounding the impact of divorce on mental health professionals:

1. The possibility that the therapists' personal experiences with divorce might affect their alliance and approach to working with couples.
2. The possibility that therapists' insight into their own biases around divorce will be beneficial to the therapeutic experience and outcome.
3. The possibility that family of origin experiences and faith of mental health professionals might impact their work with couples in distress.

The Research

By utilizing a qualitative research approach, my research provided data that offers a vivid picture of the real-life experiences of the clinicians wounded on the battlefield and in recovery. The depictions and findings offer insight into how to best reorganize and utilize lessons learned from this complex life crisis that is further complicated by our chosen profession. The themes identified through the data analysis could provide a framework for further exploration and development of interventions that might orchestrate a smoother transition to a more harmonious therapeutic relationship.

Throughout the course of the interviews, the level of sharing by participants varied; many participants often elaborated on their answers, providing a richer canvas and a deeper insight. All participants expressed feeling somewhat *glad* they participated in the interview; the process had provided them an opportunity to truly reflect on their experience. They were either surprised by the feelings of relief and closure that emerged during the interview or saddened by the pain that was still so easily triggered as they relived the experience. All had an appreciation for the irony that might be perceived by clients who seek their professional assistance. Additionally, all had the opinion that it was their experience that allowed them to resonate with those couples who are treading water and trying to keep the relationship afloat.

Doing a qualitative study provided the rich text from a participant that offers insight into the *person-of-the-therapist* and the importance of being mindful of the many avenues that are open to being influenced by this one life crisis. In painting the picture of the experience, the data suggested the presence of categories and themes. The categories indicated that perceptions of the clinicians were often twofold: the current perception of the divorce experience versus the past perception of the divorce experience. Multiple factors emerged that involved the influences from family of origin beliefs, the presence of children in the relationship, community responses to the divorce, and hope from experiencing newfound relationships.

With the exploration of the data, several themes arose. Each review of the data illuminated more clearly the existence of significant underlying themes that resonated with each participant. The six emergent themes developed as follows: (1) empathy/understanding,

INTRODUCTION

(2) creating an alliance, (3) changes/expansions in previously held views, (4) self-awareness and recovery, (5) credibility, and (6) being human and vulnerable. The themes that were teased from the data are woven into a communal fabric of the human experience of this life event.

In navigating the waters of providing effective therapy, my goal in the research was to identify common themes that become blocks to a successful therapeutic outcome, like rogue waves that knock the therapy experience off course. Most of the themes that emerged from the interviews were in fact themes that had emerged in my own experience.

THEMES

Theme One: Empathy and Understanding

Attunement and empathy allow humans to engage and respond to each other; humans are most comforted in relationships when they are understood and seen by others. The therapeutic relationship is most effective when there is a connection in which the client feels understood by a clinician expressing empathy and support. All participants revealed that their divorce experiences provided them with the ability to have a greater understanding of clients who are struggling in relationships and to have more empathy for their pain. Often, participants felt that they would have a "very different perspective" if they had not experienced their own divorce. Some of the participants felt they would not be able to provide counseling in the same way had it not been for their divorce experience. Previous research supports this conclusion that the wounds of the clinician do in fact contribute to their "humanity" and ability to empathize with others (Martin, 2011).

Theme Two: Creating an Alliance

The alliance in a counseling relationship is crucial in producing a positive experience for the client and the therapist (Bartle-Haring,

Shannon, Bowers & Holowacz, 2016; Blow, Sprenkle & Davis, 2007; Brown & O'Leary, 2000; Gellhaus Thomas, Werner-Wilson & Murphy, 2005). Forming that alliance can be complicated enough without adding the weight of the clinicians' personal relationship status. Some participants shared feelings of concern about disclosing they had been divorced. Whether disclosed or not, the participants felt they are able to connect and foster alliance because of their own pain and experience of divorce.

The frequency of disclosing the information varied with the participants; however, all agreed that the disclosure was always to benefit the client and the relationship. There are of course occasions when disclosing a past divorce does not have a beneficial impact on a therapeutic alliance; there can be very rigid ideas of acceptability for those chosen to give advice. Faith can often influence beliefs about whom we choose to seek counsel from. A few of the participants expressed having some concerns that being a divorced clinician might have a negative impact on the therapeutic relationship with clients with conservative spiritual beliefs. Previous research supports the importance of being mindful of the purpose of self-disclosure by the therapist (Karson & Fox, 2010; Kooperman, 2013). All participants identified at least one occasion where utilizing disclosure of the information was needed in order to benefit the client and/or the therapeutic relationship.

If a goal in the counseling process is to have empathy for the client, having experienced the same pain and emotions provides a clearer picture of the human experience of divorce. As noted in other research by Gerson (1996), any life crisis has the potential to impact the therapeutic alliance. In one particular situation, the clinician felt that he would have totally lost the alliance had he not shared that he understood his client's pain of having a spouse that wanted to leave the relationship. Some participants have experienced responses that negatively impacted the alliance; however, the alliance was most often improved with the disclosure of the divorce experience.

INTRODUCTION

Theme Three: Credibility or Wisdom

A *close cousin* to alliance is credibility. Creating a strong alliance requires the client have a faith that the clinician is *credible* in their ability to offer competent counseling. Having experience in the divorce process can be seen as both a negative and a positive factor in being a credible couples counselor; questions of doubt can emerge for both the client and clinician. In the data analysis, it became clear that *not* all participants felt that the disclosing the divorce experience had a negative impact on their credibility.

Many of the participants question if clients will consider them to be qualified to help couples to successfully navigate their conflict if they were not able to successfully navigate their own relationship issues. Prior research examines expectations of clients around the personal experiences and beliefs of the therapist (Tambling, Wong & Anderson, 2014). Not only do clients have expectations for therapists, but the therapists themselves often expressed feeling they should have been able to "do it better." Some of the participants have at times questioned their own competence when considering their "failure" at maintaining their relationships; none are blind to the irony and dilemma of the experience.

Theme Four: Expansion in Previously Held Views and Beliefs

The morals, values, and religious faith that we share with family of origin can be so ingrained into our being that our body can have a visceral response when we make decisions that go against our *core fiber*. Additionally, our moral beliefs are forged by the teachings of our *tribes*, showing us which behaviors are acceptable and not acceptable. Until experiencing their own divorce, most participants held beliefs or ideas about divorce that stemmed from their families of origin. Some were raised in families that had experienced generations of divorces that did not result in total destruction of the family, so divorce was not necessarily *taboo* for them.

In our families of origin, we absorb those values and strongly held beliefs of right and wrong. As we move into our own world outside of the family, sometimes our reality directly conflicts with what we have been taught, and we are forced to somehow reconcile the differences. Participants agreed that the divorce experience had at least "expanded" their views. For all participants, it was life changing in both positive and negative ways. For some of the participants, the experience changed not just one, but many important aspects of their lives; changes from spiritual beliefs, to approaches and or philosophy in their work, to views surrounding the acceptance of divorce. Some experienced shame and guilt, and for some it was devastating and yet liberating. Additionally, those that had the good fortune of experiencing a new successful relationship found a sense of hope that they could share with clients. As mental health professionals, we are ethically bound to utilize bracketing to prevent any infiltration of those past or present values and beliefs from entering the counseling experience (Ivey, D'Andrea, Ivey & Simek-Morgan, 2007; Pack-Brown, Thomas & Seymour, 2008).

Theme Five: Self-Awareness

Being present in the therapeutic process requires the clinician to be continually checking in with their emotions; paying close attention to any subtle changes that might occur as they are in session with clients. For a mental health professional, this process has at times been referred to as *person-of-the-therapist*. This *exploration* of *self* is an integral element in being effective and avoiding issues that might infiltrate and damage the therapeutic relationship. Self-awareness is achieved through self-exploration.

The majority of participants did seek out personal counseling at the time of the divorce and they continue with personal counseling today. For some, the experiences of their counseling provided insight into what did not help them to become more self-aware in their relationships. What did seem to be most helpful for all the participants

INTRODUCTION

was the knowledge gained through their training and supervision as mental health professionals. With the knowledge came the insight into their own feelings, behaviors, and roles in relationships.

Theme Six: Human and Vulnerable

Clients often see therapists as experts who have the ability to communicate in a manner that always exudes eloquence and calm. If clients keep the therapist on this pedestal, their willingness to share might be hindered by their thoughts of being too imperfect; they might feel as though they are too *crazy* or *broken* to share their story. In my own work, I often share with clients that I make mistakes, get triggered, and don't communicate in a calm *therapeutic* manner when it comes to my personal relationships; their response is always a sigh of relief. If clients view the therapist as human, does that help them to feel safe in sharing their own vulnerabilities? All of the participants in my research have at one time or another disclosed they had been divorced to at least a few clients. For the most part, they found that by sharing the experience, clients expressed feeling this somehow made them "more human" or "relatable."

Research has addressed the creation of common signature themes that stem from the life struggles that satiate the human core needs (Aponte & Kissil, 2014; Stone, 2008). Finding the commonality in the struggles helps shape the individual to empathize and understand the pain and sadness experienced by the other. Participants experienced having clients validate that seeing their "humanity" and "vulnerability" helped to establish a more comfortable and authentic therapeutic relationship. Knowing that the counselor can make the same mistakes as the client seems to provide a sense of relief and often resulted in a renewal of hope for the client. Seeing the therapist as a human who understands and makes mistakes removes some of the guilt and shame from the client.

In previous literature, similar themes did emerge addressing issues of disclosure, recovery, countertransference, transference, empathy,

9

alliance, self-doubt, considerations of children involved, and divorce adjustment (Ahrons, 1994; Basescu, 2009; Emery, 1994; Krumrei, Coit, Martin, Fogo & Mahoney, 2007; Olmstead, Blick & Mills, 2009; Ostroff, 2012; Wang & Amato, 2000). It is clear that it is incumbent upon the therapist to *do their own work* and bracket out, to the best of their ability, any influences from past or present experiences that might negatively impact their work with clients. Additionally, there is an awareness that each life experience can produce changes that can benefit the therapeutic alliance and ultimate outcome.

CHAPTER 1

"BEING" A MENTAL HEALTH PROFESSIONAL

HISTORY OF COUNSELING

Throughout the 1900s, many professions have been established that provide mental health and/or counseling services. Each profession has different levels of education, certifications, and credentialing required in order to *hang your shingle* and practice as a professional. Most of the professions also have governing bodies that determine requirements for licensure. Additionally, there exists a diverse array of counseling theories and trainings leading to a counseling process that resembles a multicolored tapestry. Depending on the therapist's educational background, theory, or framework utilized, the counseling process can look very different. In spite of all of this diversity, the overall goal of the counseling process is to help clients improve their lives through insight and change (Lambert, Bergin & Garfield, 2004).

Since the early 1800s, the field of Psychiatry has been recognized as *the profession* that provides treatment of mental illnesses. The field of psychology began in 1879, with the first experimental laboratory in psychology opened at the University of Leipzig in Germany by Wilhelm Wundt. This was followed by one of Wundt's students, G. Stanley Hall, establishing the first American experimental psychology laboratory at Johns Hopkins University in 1983 (Wertheimer, 2011).

In 1886, Joseph Jastrow received the first doctorate degree in psychology in the United States, and by 1892, the American Psychological Association was founded (Hull, 1944).

In the 20th century it was Dr. Sigmund Freud who began to transition psychiatry from a field of simply treating neurosis in patients into a process of providing long-term psychoanalysis for patients (Wertheimer, 2011). The classic vision of mental health therapy was a client lying on the couch, with the therapist sitting in a chair either behind or off to the side. The goal of the session was for the doctor to analyze the client's dreams, fantasies, and/or neurosis in order to interpret for the patient the causes of the patient's distress. This form of counseling/therapy, better known as analysis, required patients to commit to countless hours of exploration into childhood relationships and repressed sexual associations (Wertheimer, 2011).

In the early 1940s, vocational counseling services were in high demand by the government, and the profession was more widely accepted and supported. By the late 1940s, pioneers such as Maslow, Skinner, Beck, and Ellis focused research and practice from a more humanistic approach. Attention was being given to the present state of the individual. Behavioral and humanist models encouraged therapists to work from a stance of helping patients with personal growth and not dwelling solely on past experiences (Gladding, 2000).

Carl Rogers theorized that the therapist/client relationship is itself the tool to a successful outcome (Rogers, 1957). His focus was to build the relationship with the client and not simply provide vocational resources or analysis. The concept was that the therapists' ability to be empathetic, congruent, and genuine, while showing unconditional positive regard, would facilitate the growth that clients needed to create a change (Rogers, 1957). This new concept emphasized that creating a therapeutic relationship actually supersedes the therapeutic techniques utilized; this is a concept that has been debated by other researchers (Baldwin, Wampold & Imel, 2007; Norcross & Wampold, 2011; Wosket, 1999; Zuroff & Blatt, 2006). Consequently, any personal life events experienced by the therapist have the potential to significantly impact the therapists' ability to create and maintain a therapeutic alliance and relationship (Gerson, 1996).

Currently, what is referred to as couples counseling or couples therapy has also been referred to as pre-marital, marital, conjoint, collaborative, or family counseling (Broderick & Schrader, 1991; Sager, 1966). With an underlying foundation in systems and attachment theory, the focus of therapy tended to be on the entire system versus separating out the couple (Gurman & Fraenkel, 2002). In current society, there is a diverse population of partners who seek couples counseling; what now constitutes a couple can be any two individuals in a relationship. The diversity and variations may have a significant impact on the therapeutic relationship for both the therapist and the client (Jacobson & Addis, 1993).

Reviewing the history of couples counseling, there does not seem to be a consensus on when the field originated (Gurman & Fraenkel, 2002; Sager, 1966). Regardless of the actual origination of the therapy for couples, currently approximately one half of married couples in the United States are experiencing distress in their relationship, and approximately one third of those in distress will seek couples counseling (Doss et al., 2016). Gottman, Johnson, Hendrix, and many more—there are several different theoretical approaches that have been researched for effectiveness and are utilized by therapists working with couples (Baucom, Atkins, Rowe, Doss & Christensen, 2015; Busby & Holman, 2009; Byrne, Carr & Clark, 2004; Christensen, Atkins, Baucom & Yi, 2010; Cookerly, 1980; Efron & Bradley, 2007; Greenberg & Johnson, 1986; Gottman & Krokoff, 1989; Jacobson, Christensen, Prince, Cordova & Eldridge, 2000; Snyder, Mangrum & Wills, 1993). By examining the outcome or success in utilizing these methods in counseling, research shows that the field of couples counseling does have a positive impact on relieving distress and promoting a healthier relationship for the couple (Baucom & Hoffman, 1986; Beckerman & Sarracco, 2002; Bray & Jouriles, 1995; Gottman & Gottman, 1999; Greenman & Johnson, 2013; Hafen & Crane, 2003;

Holliman, Muro & Luquet, 2016; Johnson & Talitman, 1997; Snyder, Wills & Grady-Fletcher, 1991).

In a plenary address at the 2006 Emotionally Focused Therapy Summit, Dr. Sue Johnson cited a 2004 poll in *Psychology Today* that identified "difficulties with a partner" as the most stressful event in the life of an individual. Johnson (2007) notes that conflicts with a partner actually ranked higher than the stress of medical issues. Research supports that being in a healthy couples relationship impacts each individual's overall good health and well-being (Booth & Amato, 1991; Kiecolt-Glaser & Newton, 2001; Proulx, Helms & Buehler, 2007). Additionally, it increases lifespan (Johnson, Backlund, Sorlie & Loveless, 2000) and decreases absenteeism in the workplace (Markussen, Røed, Røgeberg & Gaure, 2011). The importance of couples therapy to current society is further underscored by the fact that in North America, issues with a partner are the primary reason people seek out any psychological therapy (Johnson, 2007).

The Counseling Process—The Research of Getting It Right

The *process* of counseling is a *shared experience* through which the trained and objective mental health professional guides the client to find insight into their journey without bringing our own personal road bumps into the session. When the mental health professional is in shock or badly bruised from a marriage that has crashed and burned, what impact does it have on their ability to provide effective counseling to couples? As with other areas of counseling, working with couples in distress might trigger many of the therapists' own wounds from their personal relationships. Once triggered, the emotional reaction has the potential to impact the therapist's ability to counsel from a place of neutrality. Maintaining this neutrality requires therapists to be persistent in examining their own feelings and biases. Therapists have a duty to be attuned and vigilant in identifying when their own personal issues impact their work with a client (Aponte & Carlson, 2009; Aponte & Kissil, 2014; Cheon & Murphy, 2007).

The therapeutic relationship is mutual, interactive, and dynamic, with the potential to have many variables shaping the flow. Numerous studies in mental health counseling have focused on identifying variables that might influence the outcome of counseling (Lambert et al., 2004; Nelson, Heilbrun & Figley, 1993; Sanberk & Akbaş, 2015; Wampold, 2001).

Over the years, many researchers have examined the need human beings have to connect and exist in relationships: a craving to be social creatures with a tendency to attach and function as a system (Minuchin, Rosman & Baker, 1978; Nicoll, 1993; Parsons, 1951; Radcliff-Brown, 1952; Werner, Altman, Oxley & Haggard, 1987). From a systemic framework, the therapist theoretically becomes a part of the system in the counseling relationship. As part of the system, the therapist's beliefs, values, attitudes, spirituality, social views, and culture have the potential to impact the other members in that system (Aponte & Carlsen, 2009; Gelso, 2011; McDowell & Shelton, 2002). The influence of those values depends on the weight placed on those issues. Issues such as religion, infidelity, and age of children might be valued by the therapist and hence affect the interventions and options offered to the couple (Butler, Rodriguez, Roper & Feinauer, 2010; Kalter & Rembar, 1981; Olmstead et al., 2009; Shafranske, 1996; Softas-Nall, Beadle, Newell & Helm, 2008). Keeping in mind my own biases and *self-of-the-therapist* work, I am cognizant of the potential influence of my own experiences with divorce and the potential influence on the system when working with clients and conducting this research.

In Swanson's 2004 dissertation, he focused on the experience of divorce in a population of young men. The participants' divorce experiences were identified as a "crucible" in their development. The Merriam-Webster Dictionary (2017) defines crucible as a "difficult test or challenge" and a "place or situation that forces people to change or make difficult decisions." I believe that my research sought to examine the possible *forced changes* that might occur for divorced therapists who are committed to working with couples and families and to explore the mental health professionals' own personal experience with divorce and how this life crisis might ultimately influence the interventions and direction of their work with couples.

Some researchers have focused on the impact of the professional training experience itself, both the personal and professional life of the therapist (Montagno, Svatovic & Levenson, 2011; Niño, Kissil & Apolinar-Claudio, 2015; Wetzler, Frame & Litzinger, 2011). Others have focused on the counseling process and exploring the reasons and techniques necessary for achieving a successful outcome (Gelso & Hayes, 2002; Gelso & Hayes, 2007; Sharma & Fowler, 2016; Wallerstein, 1990). Additional research has examined a variety of issues for therapists in their work with clients: self-disclosure, gender, attitudes towards divorce, therapists' perspectives on alliance, and therapists in crisis (Aponte & Carlsen, 2009; Kooperman, 2013; Mathews, 1988; Nissen-Lie, Havik, Høglend, Rønnestad, & Monsen, 2014).

A quantitative study by Ostroff (2012) reported that a majority of the divorced therapists were able to identify more positive effects than negative effects in their life. The data also identified that therapists experienced an increase in strength, compassion, empathy, and sensitivity from their own divorce experience. Additionally, therapists reported that they noticed an increased interest in their counseling work for months after their divorce. Other issues discussed in the research were countertransference, empathy, values, and beliefs when working with clients that might have been influenced by their own experience of divorce in their family.

There is an abundance of research examining client-therapist interactions and the factors that influence the therapeutic relationship. However, there are differing opinions as to whether it is the client or the therapist that most impacts the relationship (Berry et al., 2015; Hadžiahmetović, Alispahić, Tuce & Hasanbegović-Anić, 2016). Recent research examining clients with depression discussed the concept of the *patient-therapist* or *client-therapist* relationship as being bi-directional (Ahola et al., 2011; Aponte & Kissil, 2014). Research has identified clients' factors that contributed to success in the counseling process. A study by Sanberk and Akbaş (2015) found that clients' behaviors such as emotional disclosure, cooperation, participation in the process, and ability to express change contributed to therapists reporting a more successful counseling experience. If the therapist and client have differing personal beliefs regarding divorce, does that impact the ability of the therapist to show empathy and supportive behaviors to the client? Furthermore, if the client experiences a difference in beliefs around divorce, does this inhibit the client's ability to feel safe enough to disclose emotions and feelings?

Overall, the number one factor shown to influence the outcome of therapy is the alliance between the client and therapist (Bartle-Haring et al., 2016; Blow et al., 2007; Brown & O'Leary, 2000; Gellhaus Thomas et al., 2005). This alliance relies heavily on the clinicians' ability to be emotionally attuned, genuine, and present with clients (Johnson, 2007; Montagno et al., 2011; Rogers, 1957). Other elements of counseling that have been examined to impact the alliance are being present, maintaining attunement, and monitoring disclosure with clients during a session (Aponte & Kissil, 2014; Counselman & Alonso, 1993; Kooperman, 2013; Sharma & Fowler, 2016). Hence, therapists who are experiencing their own personal life crises might experience difficulties with a variety of those critical elements in working with clients.

The therapeutic alliance has been researched extensively as a key factor in predicting a successful outcome in therapy (Bartle-Haring et al., 2016; Blow et al., 2007; Brown & O'Leary, 2000; Gellhaus Thomas et al., 2005; Kim, Wampold & Bolt, 2006; Mamodhoussen, Wright, Tremblay & Poitras-Wright, 2005; Martin, Garske & Davis, 2000). Results of the research indicated that the use of different therapy methods has a significantly lesser effect on the clients' experience of the counseling and outcome versus the aspects of the individual clinician and the quality of the alliance (Benish, Imel & Wampold, 2008; Blatt, Zuroff, & Pilkonis, 1996; Kim et al., 2006; Safran, Muran & Proskurov, 2008). One study suggested that when working with couples, the alliance between client and therapist is perceived differently by males and females, and is also directly correlated to the alliance between the partners (Anker, Owen, Duncan & Sparks, 2010).

Research also indicates that the creation of the alliance is more dependent on the therapists' personal characteristics and quality of life than the therapists' professional qualifications and model of therapy utilized with clients (Benish et al., 2008; Blatt, Sanislow, Zuroff & Pilkonis, 1996; Bohart, Elliott, Greenberg & Watson, 2002; Nissen-Lie, Havik, Høglend, Monsen & Rønnestad, 2013; Rogers, 1957; Safran et al., 2008; Sanberk & Akbaş, 2015; Simon, 2012). When the therapist's personal experiences are stressful or painful enough to interfere with the activities of daily living or quality of life, there is a possibility that the event can easily influence that therapeutic relationship. In research by Nissen-Lie et al. (2013), findings indicated that the therapists' quality of life is a significant factor in creating and maintaining the working alliance between a client and therapist. With this in mind, the therapist should take into consideration whether a break is necessary for recovery from the crisis. Does the crisis result in a *trauma response* that impacts their quality of life and ability to be fully present and effective in a therapy session?

A study examining theoretical approach and the alliance suggested that the framework or approach may in fact impact the therapeutic alliance (Stevens, Muran, Safran, Gorman & Winston, 2007). According to Sanberk and Akbaş (2015), the behaviors of therapists and clients mutually affect each other during the counseling process. Therapists' behaviors are heavily influenced by their choice of a therapeutic framework. This framework, usually chosen during the training process, is integral in relation to the counseling process. If the process of counseling is a mutual exchange of information and emotions, it is valuable to explore whether the variable of framework and/or training affects the exchange.

Two factors that have been researched in establishing a therapeutic alliance are collaboration and having an empathetic engagement in the therapeutic process (Castonguay & Beutler, 2006; Karson & Fox, 2010). The therapist's emotional connection with the client and engagement in the process were shown to substantially activate the emotional connection by the client (Friedlander, Lambert, Valentín & Cragun, 2008). Furthermore, when clients displayed behaviors that would not be considered collaborative, the therapist tended to utilize interventions that did not promote a connection. This resulted in blocks in building alliances during a session. Other research indicated that if the therapist is uncomfortable with a client's behaviors or responses, the therapist forgoes attunement with the client, and focuses more on tasks in the treatment plan. This can lead to issues around countertransference as well power and control of sessions (Sharma & Fowler, 2016).

The concept of *person-of-the-therapist* or *self-of-the-therapist* has been researched in an effort to gain understanding of how the *variable* of the therapist as a human being influences the creation of the therapeutic alliance and ultimately the outcome of the therapy (Aponte & Carlsen, 2009; Aponte & Kissil, 2014; Baldwin, 2000; Blow et al., 2007; Cheon & Murphy, 2007; Nelson et al., 1993). Often, therapists are experiencing many of the same life events as their clients. As mental health professionals examine the impact of crises on the life of the client, it is crucial to also explore the impact of their own crisis in order to gain understanding of how these life events might influence the therapists' work with a client (Butler et al., 2010; Cheon & Murphy, 2007; Kooperman, 2013; Rober, 2011; Shane, 2002).

Aponte and Carlsen (2009) proposed that everyone has underlying core needs that create signature themes in their lives. These themes identify each person's unique lifelong struggles and are referred to as "signature themes." These struggles are responsible for shaping the relationship the individual has with the self and with others. It is proposed that these themes are so universal that they allow therapists to empathize and connect with clients enough to provide effective counseling (Aponte & Kissil, 2014; Stone, 2008).

A meta-analysis of therapeutic outcome studies revealed that the *person-of-the-therapist* and the therapeutic alliance are the two main components that contribute to client satisfaction with counseling

(Wampold, 2001). As human beings, we all face each day with wounds of our past relationships; mental health professionals are no different than non-professionals. Previous research has nicknamed those in the arena of counseling as "wounded healers" (Aponte & Kissil, 2014; Martin, 2011; Miller & Baldwin, 2013; Stone, 2008). How clinicians utilize their wounds, or core issues, in a therapy session is a critical element that extends beyond the techniques and skills learned in the classroom (Aponte & Kissil, 2014; Martin, 2011; Rober, 2011). Successful therapists achieve a level of competency in identifying and acknowledging emotions and reactions surrounding their wounds, while maintaining the ability to utilize these experiences in order to empathize with clients. Some researchers consider therapists' wounds to be the element that provides them with a sense of humanity that opens the door to empathy (Martin, 2011).

The *person-of-the-therapist* is proposed to be an integral factor in the therapeutic relationship (Aponte & Kissil, 2014; Blow et al., 2007; Wampold, 2001). A therapist's personal qualities, as well as life conditions and personal crises, all affect the therapists' interactions and work with clients (Nissen-Lie et al., 2013). The values and beliefs of both the therapist and the client have the potential to play a role in alliance in the therapeutic relationship (Gellhaus Thomas et al., 2005; Sharma & Fowler, 2016). The human being who is *person-of-the-therapist*, might experience challenges in neutrality if values and beliefs are totally contrary to those of the client.

For the therapist, identifying personal wounds and addressing the impact of those wounds in the therapeutic process is key to avoiding variables that have a negative impact on the therapeutic relationship (Baldwin, 2000; Aponte & Kissil, 2014). Identifying issues stemming from family of origin are just as important for therapists as clients. The exploration of these experiences can be challenging but is critical to identifying the impact on the *person-of-the-therapist* (Gerson, 1996). Additionally, as therapists are experiencing their own life crises, there needs to be an awareness of how the emotions and stressors associated with those events are influencing their own work with clients. Many researchers have focused on therapists' ability to effectively attend to their own needs and issues in order to effectively work with clients (Gelso & Hayes, 2007; Rønnestad & Skovholt, 2012; Skovholt & Jennings, 2004).

Research does indicate that any personal life crises experienced by therapists do, in some way, impact their work with clients (Al-Mateen, 1991; Counselman & Alonso, 1993; Deutsch, 1985; Kooperman, 2013). Several studies have looked at the impact of illness on therapists (Abend, 1982; Grunebaum, 1993; Guy & Souder, 1986; Morrison, 1990). Research that explored the impact of death of a family member has reported that some clients might see the therapist as "invulnerable" to the unexpected life crises that are experienced by others (Givelber & Simon, 1981). Several researchers have examined the impact of divorce in the life of a therapist and found that divorce can have both positive and negative consequences (Acock & Demo, 1994; Ahrons, 1994; Basescu, 2009; Johansen, 1993; Pappas, 1989; Riessman, 1990; Schlachet, 1996). A study by Clemente-Crain (1996) reported findings from interviews of psychotherapists who experienced divorce in their families of origin. The participants reported that the divorce had in some fashion shaped their work with clients.

Additional research has examined the *divorce adjustment* period and paints a portrait of what a *well-adjusted* divorced individual should resemble (Kitson, 1992; Krumrei et al., 2007; Wang & Amato, 2000). For the most part, all agree that a *well-adjusted* post-divorce individual is one who is able to accept the divorce and not continue to experience strong negative feelings surrounding the divorce or ex-spouse. A study by Emery (1994) suggested that the person who initiated the divorce usually adjusts better to the actual divorce because they have experienced the stressful period prior to the actual divorce. Some research found that having a positive intimate relationship post-divorce was "significantly" associated with a more positive divorce adjustment (Wang & Amato, 2000).

Some research examined the impact of specific issues surrounding the therapist and marriage counseling. Issues such as ages of the children; therapists' personal experiences with divorce, infidelity, or violence in the relationship; and the therapists' view of a successful outcome with couples therapy have been examined (Butler et al., 2010; Kalter & Rembar, 1981; Levengood, Ottaviano & Chambliss, 1996; Olmstead et al., 2009; Sabatelli & Bartle-Haring, 2003; Softas-Nall et al., 2008). Research by Levengood et al. (1996) found that a therapist would utilize more interventions in support of the option of divorce if the therapist possessed a greater knowledge of divorce impacting children with possible positive effects. The study suggested that this phenomenon is possibly related to therapists' own positive experiences with divorce.

Another factor previously examined is that of the expectations held by clients and how that expectation might influence the outcome of therapy (Aubuchon-Endsley, Callahan & Scott, 2014; Myers & Truluck, 1998). The research explored the clients' expectations about perceived roles and values of the therapist. Research has consistently revealed that clients enter into the therapeutic process with expectations around the therapist, the method, and the outcome (Aubuchon-Endsley et al., 2014; Glass, Arnkoff & Shapiro, 2001; Joyce, Ogrodniczuk, Piper & McCallum, 2003; Tambling & Johnson, 2010). Additional research examined the clients' *role expectations* of the therapist and the therapists' actual behaviors. Findings indicated that clients reported experiencing a more robust therapeutic alliance and identified a more positive outcome of the therapy when the expectations and behaviors matched (Aubuchon-Endsley et al., 2014; Patterson, Uhlin & Anderson, 2008).

Research on Native American clients identifies a belief that this population might have expectations of outcomes that are different than other cultures (Aubuchon-Endsley et al., 2014). This research highlighted the possibility that due to cultural beliefs, the population's expectation is that therapists will draw from their own personal life lessons. If there is in fact an expectation in some cultures that therapists will be drawing on their own personal life lessons, what does that mean for therapists who are drawing on lessons learned about the experience of divorce?

Other research suggests that clients identify therapists' interpersonal qualities and interpersonal functioning in their personal lives as more pertinent to the therapeutic alliance (Anderson, Ogles, Pattersen, Lambert & Vermeersch, 2009; Simon, 2012). Qualities such as empathy, supportive behaviors, affirmativeness, compassion, and responsiveness are reported as being valued by clients in forming an alliance. Furthermore, the interpersonal qualities of counselors are also more significant to clients than their theoretical orientation, type of training, and level of experience (Bohart et al., 2002; Karson & Fox, 2010; Nissen-Lie et al., 2013; Sanberk & Akbaş, 2015).

Grunebaum (1993) examined therapists who had been injured or experienced an illness. His findings revealed that many of the therapists reported feeling a need to return to work possibly sooner than optimal due to concerns about income, having "high standards" for themselves, and wanting to avoid feeling guilt around neglecting clients. The therapists also identified feeling that returning to work improved their self-esteem. The research discussed that this decision to resume work too soon after the crisis might have resulted in the therapist being more vulnerable to countertransference, inability to be present, and over-disclosing in an attempt to receive "validation and comfort" from the client.

When therapists experience a life crisis, whether or not they disclose this information, clients might non-verbally receive the message. Research indicates that through a therapist's non-verbal communication, a client can sense when a therapist is experiencing a distressful period in their private life (Gerson, 1996; Håvås, Svartberg & Ulvenes, 2015). The non-verbal skill of attunement helps therapists connect with clients and supports the creation of the alliance. At the same time, clients become attuned to the therapist and may pick up on the body language of the therapist. Ramseyer and Tschacher (2011) explored non-verbal synchrony in therapist/client body movements. The data in this study supports an enhanced quality of the relationship and more successful outcomes in therapy when the therapist/client body movements are in synchrony. When the therapist is experiencing a personal life crisis, the body language alone might express the stress to client.

Often, therapists are experiencing many of the same life events as their clients. As therapists are exploring the impact of crises on the life of the client, it is beneficial for therapists to also explore the impact of their own crisis in order to gain understanding of how these life events might influence the therapists' work with a client (Butler et al., 2010; Cheon & Murphy, 2007; Kooperman, 2013; Rober, 2011; Shane, 2002). Gerson (1996) compiled stories from a variety of therapists sharing their own *person-of-the-therapist* experiences with life crisis. One discussion in the book addresses the experience of divorce in the life of a therapist. Schlachet (pp. 141–157) explores how his personal life crisis of divorce impacted the attunement with his clients. Despite not disclosing his marital struggles, he received many questions from his clients regarding his well-being. According to Schlachet, his clients sensed his lack of engagement and presence in the sessions. This experience reinforces the proposal that when something impacts therapists' quality of life, their clients sense a disruption in exchanges in the relationship.

Do clients look for a mental health professional with similar religious beliefs and views on marriage? Previous literature suggests that the religious beliefs of clients should be considered as an appropriate topic of discussion in the counseling sessions, as this might impact both the therapist and client in the therapeutic relationship (Koenig, 1998; Miovic et al., 2006; Richards & Bergin, 2000; Rose, Westefeld & Ansely, 2001; Shafranske, 1996; Walker, Gorsuch & Tan, 2005). Some research suggested that clients actually expect that during the course of counseling sessions, the counselor will employ religious interventions (Martinez, Smith & Barlow, 2007; Post, Wade & Cornish, 2014; Wade, Worthington & Vogel, 2007). However, differences in the religious beliefs of therapists and clients should not determine whether or not the therapist meets with a client (Kocet & Herlihy, 2014).

In a study that compared secular versus religiously affiliated sites, more secular therapists focused on the well-being of the individual, whereas therapists working in religious affiliated agencies focused more on the family. Secular therapists also tended to view their role as more of a neutral mediator (Winters et al., 1995). This research also suggests that the secular therapists more often utilized questions around forgiveness and love versus their non-secular counterpart. Other research examined Christian counselors and beliefs about sex and relationships (Sanders, Swenson & Schneller, 2011).

When a difference in values or religious beliefs exists between the therapist and the client, it is the responsibility of the therapist to be mindful of these differences when providing counseling (Kitchener & Anderson, 2011; Kocet & Herlihy, 2014; Pope & Vasquez, 2011). In order to accomplish the goal of bracketing, therapists must be able to suspend their own personal feelings and values in order to prevent these elements from interfering with a counseling session (Evans, Kincade & Seem, 2011; Kocet & Herlihy, 2014). As a mental health professional working with couples in distress, it is imperative to have the ability to identify personal feelings and beliefs surrounding the complex issues of couples and divorce. Any impairment in this arena risks the alliance and ultimately the therapeutic outcome.

Bracketing has been long been utilized in qualitative research to encourage researchers to pre-emptively identify and explore their own biases prior to meeting with participants involved in the study (Marshall & Rossman, 2011). In the counseling process, therapists should work to prevent any interference by their own values and experiences by utilizing the tactic of ethical bracketing. This skill has been proposed as essential process (Kocet & Herlihy, 2014). Research in multicultural counseling supported the idea that biases in counseling may be unethical and ineffective and have potentially harmful effects on clients (Ivey et al., 2007; Pack-Brown et al., 2008).

The importance of bracketing is not unique to the mental health profession; other health care professions have also focused research on the concept of bracketing in providing care and avoiding potential harmful effects to patients (Fletcher, 2015; Garroutte, Sarkisian, Goldberg, Buchwald & Beals, 2008; Kilgour, Kosny, McKenzie &

Collie, 2015; Shetty et al., 2016). Mental health professionals are ethically bound to *do no harm* to clients. It is the ethical duty of professional therapists to provide effective and non-judgmental counseling. However, as human beings, all mental health professionals bring their own biases into the counseling session. Mental health professionals should be cognizant of their abilities and limitations in bracketing the impacts of a personal life crisis.

Over the years, counseling research has focused on the subject of transference and countertransference in the therapist/client relationship (Abend, 1982; Fuertes, Gelso, Owen & Cheng, 2013; Hayes, Gelso & Hummel, 2011; Marmarosh et al., 2009). A previous study reported that when a therapist maintains an agenda focused on accomplishing tasks, or is avoidant of certain topics, the entire therapeutic process is possibly hindered by both transference and countertransference (Sharma & Fowler, 2016). Essentially, the manner in which therapists guide the topics of discussion may in fact be a result of countertransference issues.

Research conducted by Wallerstein (1990) examined the relationship of transference and countertransference in therapists working with divorcing couples. She proposed that the therapeutic alliance directly depends on the therapist's experiences and ability to resonate with the experiences of the client. Furthermore, due to the intense emotions involved in romantic relationships and divorce, a therapist is more likely to experience countertransference issues when working with divorcing couples. Additionally, Wallerstein (1990) discussed findings that show differences with the issues of transference by the client based on gender.

Previous research further examined and suggested that when therapists are in distress, factors such as their ability to manage countertransference is affected, as well as the ability to self-reflect (Gelso & Hayes, 2002; Gelso & Hayes, 2007; Rønnestad & Skovholt, 2012; Skovholt & Jennings, 2004). When the ability to self-reflect and manage countertransference does not occur, the therapeutic relationship cannot escape the impact. Researchers have also examined the particular personal stress factors such as the impact of therapists' illness (Counselman & Alonso, 1993), pregnancy (Al-Mateen, 1991), and a therapist experiencing a personal crisis (Kooperman, 2013).

Shane (2002) explored the effect of a therapist's divorce on the therapeutic relationship. She describes divorce as a "transformative" experience for a therapist in the analytic process. In the article, she explored the impact of her own divorce on her function as an analyst as well as the impact on her clients. Shane also examined the process of self-disclosure in the therapeutic relationship and the impact of personal disclosure with her clients. The question is not whether there is an impact; it is simply a question of how much of an impact actually occurs. When a client learns of the therapist's divorce, does their empathy for the therapist distract the client from focusing on their own issues?

Gender has been researched as a potential factor in clients' expectations of a successful therapeutic process (Hardin & Yanico, 1983; Raylu & Kaur, 2012). Overall, females tend to have higher expectations for counseling outcomes. However, males have an expectation that the clinician be an "expert," participate in self-disclosure, and be more straightforward in their approach (Tinsley, Workman & Kass, 1980). This may indicate that males seek advice to solve situations based on the therapists' own personal experiences (Hardin & Yanico, 1983; Raylu & Kaur, 2012).

Clients seek counseling services with expectations that mental health professionals have the answers and solutions to their problems. Previous research focusing on therapeutic outcomes suggests that the clients' expectations of the therapist and of the therapeutic process might be an additional factor in the creation of the alliance (Aubuchon-Endsley et al., 2014; Glass et al., 2001; Tambling & Johnson, 2010). Likewise, clients have expectations regarding the personal experiences and the beliefs of the therapists that might play an important role in creating the therapeutic alliance (Rose et al., 2001; Miovic et al., 2006; Tambling et al., 2014).

When humans encounter a new relationship, they utilize a method known as "relational framing" in an effort to categorize an unfamiliar situation into a familiar situation by using past experiences. This technique helps to guide the direction of the interactions and the defined roles each person should play in the relationship. Previous research examined this phenomenon and how it impacts the therapeutic relationship (Bass, 2007; Karson, 2008; Karson & Fox, 2010). Due to the uniqueness of the relationship, boundaries around disclosure are different than non-therapeutic relationships (Karson & Fox, 2010). In the therapeutic relationship, the therapist's lack of disclosure of personal information might be confusing for clients in terms of relational framing. Much research has focused on therapists' disclosure of personal information and how that impacts the alliance and the process (Karson & Fox, 2010; Mathews, 1988; Simon, 1988). In reviewing the research on disclosure, there is evidence that supports the possible positive and negative impacts of disclosure as well as the *whys* of disclosure (Basescu, 2009; Schlachet, 1996; Shane, 2002).

Disclosure of personal information is typical and expected in most relationships. However, self-disclosure is one of the elements that separate the counseling relationship from all other relationships (Greenspan, 1984; Mathews, 1988). This type of withholding of personal information by the therapist might feel unfamiliar to the clients. Additionally, clients are encouraged to disclose intimate details of their lives in an effort to explore and gain insight. The fact that this is not meant to be a reciprocal process might feel confusing for some clients.

The therapist's ability to determine the appropriate amount of self-disclosure with a client might easily be impacted by the intensity of the personal crisis being experienced. Therapists must maintain a continual process of self-awareness in order to evaluate the impact of the crisis and monitor the impact on their self-disclosure in sessions (Karson & Fox, 2010). The question to be considered is: *Does this information benefit the client?*

My research was based on the premise that the therapeutic process is an extension of the *person-of-the-therapist* and cannot escape unintended consequences of life crises experienced by mental health professionals (Aponte & Carlsen, 2009; Aponte & Kissil, 2014). Although the therapist/client relationship is a unique system, each of the participants brings *the self* into the system and impacts the system in some way. The focus of my research was an exploration of the specific personal life crisis of divorce for the mental health professional, the potential impact of the experience on the therapeutic alliance, and other aspects of the therapeutic process.

Chapter 2

OUR STORIES

I am sincerely grateful to the gracious clinicians who willingly shared their personal stories with me. In an effort to ensure their privacy is maintained, the names and some personal specifics have been changed, but the stories are true and resonate with many unnamed professionals who share similar experiences and challenges. The life stories were often painful to share and yet each reached deep to share the story of the *person-of-the-therapist*. Each shared from a place of vulnerability and honesty in offering any insight that might help other travelers who find themselves on this path.

All participants in the research have been licensed professionals for more than five years and are currently working with couples or families that include couples. Two of the participants work in agency settings and the rest have private practices. The current relationship status of the participants varied as well as the amount of time since the divorce. One of the participants was in the process of a divorce at the time of the interview while another participant had experienced the divorce 25 years ago. In fact, that participant was now in the 24th year of the second marriage. Two of the participants have been divorced twice. Five of the participants reported it was their partner who left the relationship. Only one of the participants described the divorce as "amicable" and remains friends with the ex-spouse. Three of the participants are "happy" second marriages and two others report currently being in successful committed relationships. Those participants with current successful relationships all identify feeling that those relationships have a positive impact on their work with couples.

My goal in recruiting participants was to invite a diverse population of clinicians to share their experience, including diversity in age, race, gender, education, and geographic location. There is a diversity of licensures and educational backgrounds in the mental health profession, and I recognize this factor might have an impact on the clinicians and their approach in working with clients. Addressing this diversity alone was important to me in order to avoid limiting the information collected in the data. Additionally, I believed it was important to have equal representation of males and female participants. I was able to recruit all eight participants through professional and academic affiliations. One participant actually approached me to volunteer for the study after hearing about the research through another colleague. It was surprising to me how willing the participants were to share stories of experiences that were so personal and often painful.

YOUR GUIDES ON THE JOURNEY OF ENLIGHTENMENT

Tanya
Enlightenment Can Be Painful

We have been married and divorced twice (to each other) and most of our family and friends don't notice the difference. Our relationship looks almost the same; still friends, still doing family vacations and still totally not able to get out of our cycles.

Our first marriage lasted 21 years; we had been separated twice, but each time we repaired as best we could in order to maintain the family. After being divorced for two years we remarried (for our children) and stayed together another six years. My marriages ended quietly both times; there was no blow up, no custody battles, no property disputes, and no counseling. In fact, for the second divorce, there were no lawyers. I simply printed forms I found online and, with the help of a friend, found the right officials to sign the right documents.

Our relationship has been far from tumultuous; except for our children, no one ever saw us arguing. If anything, our relationship as a couple was painfully distant and lonely. We just *did not get each other*. We were the epitome of a *Martian* and a *Venusian*, totally from different planets on opposite ends of the intensity poles. In Emotionally Focused Therapy language, I am the ultimate Pursuer and he is the definitive Withdrawer.

For many years we both knew that as a couple, we just did not connect. But, we had three beautiful children and we both loved being together as a family. We were the couple who did everything with their children. In fact, we usually had many of our friends' children with us while they went out as a couple. In the end, it was our focus on our children and what parenting *should look like* that was the impetus to the total demise of the relationship.

My first career was as a Neonatal Nurse Practitioner; I did not begin my education in counseling until immediately after the first divorce. As with most of us who are *older non-traditional* students, I agonized in Childhood Development class as I learned about all of the mistakes and damage I had inflicted on my own children. And as I sat in silence in Marriage and Family, I gained painful insight into what mistakes I had made in my own marriage.

You would think that with this newfound enlightenment, I would have been able to make the marriage work the second time around. Instead, as I was working towards my certification in Emotionally Focused Therapy, it was becoming clearer that we genuinely did not connect in the way we should. We just did not seem to agree on . . . almost anything. In my trainings, I would hear stories from other therapists who had the kind of relationships in which they had each other's back and really wanted to be with each other. I began to realize that there might be the possibility to have a relationship where two individuals *get each other and actually like each other*. It seemed possible that a couple could want to and be able to meet each other's needs. With each training, the spotlight on my own relationship only illuminated the longings that had been unfulfilled for both of us all these years in the endless cycle that we simply could not step out of. So, I decided to end the marriage again, not with a bang but a whimper.

Mary
Still Friends

My ex-husband and I were so close; we were friends and we were friends after the divorce. And I'm still close with his family and he is still close to mine. We were amicable, so I guess for me our divorce wasn't final, it didn't end our relationship.

Mary and her ex-husband had been together as a couple since the age of 14. After almost 10 years of dating, they were married for almost five years. At the time of the divorce, her children's ages were 13, 9, and 8. Although her husband had agreed to attend one couples session, "When it was time to do the counseling, he backed out." Mary was separated for almost eight months prior to the decision to divorce.

When we decided to get divorced we split for seven or eight months so we just split and then we got a divorce. It was amicable and it wasn't long or drawn out. It was like a decision and then we went through with the paper work. By the time we decided to get a divorce it was a matter of paper work. It ended our relationship as husband and wife but we co-parented and, my family and his family, we were from the same community, so we ended our marriage but we didn't end our relationship, if that makes sense.

Mary was working as a counselor at the time of her divorce and she did not take a break from working with her clients. She felt she had processed the relationship struggles long before the divorce. Mary believes that the relationship experiences with her ex-husband actually helped her with her clients. It is the experiences she has had of being married, getting divorced, and successfully co-parenting that have provided her with a perspective that she has found invaluable in providing counseling to couples and families.

Corey
What's Wrong With Me

Hard [the divorce], I guess. I had no clue what was really going on, but I was caught in one of those demon dialogues I guess. We were just . . . yeah it was rough. We really didn't have a lot of stuff to split, so the actual signing of the paperwork was easy but the emotional pain and self-doubt and all of that stuff that comes with it, that was really hard.

Corey experienced his divorce about 10 years ago. He shared that he did not want to get divorced, but ultimately, he realized it was "inevitable." Corey did not have any children at the time of the divorce. His ex-wife had an affair prior to their decision to separate. He described his divorce as "a three-year process of fighting and struggling." After the three years, his ex-wife moved out and they were "disconnected" for about a year. They had talked about going to counseling; however, neither one of them ever seemed to make time for it. During the period of separation, Corey reported that she would "randomly call," but would become defensive when he asked for clarification as to why she had left the marriage. The final decision to end the marriage was "mutual."

Despite the divorce being mutual, Corey experienced feeling "rejected and unloved," which led him to a place of self-doubt and bitterness:

> . . . and then also like having this place of questioning, 'What's wrong with me? Why did this happen? Why did I pick this person?' Umm and hindsight is 20/20, so there was 'What was I thinking?'

There were a lot of red flags before I got married that I noticed and just kind of pushed through. So, then I started thinking, 'Can I trust myself? Can I trust myself to make good decisions?' And again, kind of having that . . . Well what the heck is wrong with women and they are all kind of the same, they are after money and they just want somebody who is going to do what they want and I got pretty bitter about it.

After the divorce, it was difficult for Corey to imagine that he would find a partner who wanted to be in a *real* relationship. He and his new wife found each other while attending a graduate program for counseling. "We did pre-engagement counseling. As my wife put it, 'We both knew how to mess up a relationship' [laugh]."

Catherine
Still Trying to Detach

My divorce is a living, breathing thing that cycles back and I feel like I'm always waiting for the other shoe to drop.

Although married for 30 years, Catherine admits to having her own misgivings before the marriage; however, she convinced herself that "it would work." Even before the wedding, when a serious issue arose between Catherine and her ex-husband's parents, he was not willing to support her over the wishes of his parents. Catherine's family and friends were concerned about the relationship from the very beginning. They did not see her and her husband as a "good match" and often shared their feelings with her:

I had friends and family telling me not to marry who I did. At that point I was very young, I think I was 23, and what I heard was that they didn't think I could do it; then it was almost a challenge. I just didn't see it clearly.

As her uncle walked her down the aisle for her wedding, he said, "Well, I guess this is ok for your first marriage."

After "close to 20 years" of marriage counseling, the marriage finally ended four years ago. Catherine has five children; at the time of her divorce, her youngest child was in high school getting ready for college. She describes her divorce as "the most conflictual divorce at that time in this area, according to the judges." As for many involved in a divorce, the experience for Catherine was "arduous and traumatic."

> I was not traumatized by the separation or the detachment from my ex-husband, but by the impact on the children and also my financial. I'm getting close to retirement age and being taken down to zero, that's the part that's still sort of an ongoing legacy of that. And still he will target the children every once in a while with the money. And in my opinion, abusive behavior towards them, I don't get that anymore but they do. So that's difficult, that part is still sort of a living, breathing kind of thing.

From the time of the divorce until now, her ex-husband has brought lawsuits against her about a dozen times. She shared that her ex-husband "threatened and did bring me to bankruptcy," and almost did. Because her ex-husband continues to pursue legal actions, and manipulate the financial well-being of her children, the divorce continues to bring turmoil into her life. However, she felt that through her training in an attachment model, she has "changed her strategy in her divorce." Although she cannot "detach" from him completely, she has found it helpful to work with him in ways that provide enough "attachment" to keep matters as "calm" as possible.

Kyle
Happiness on the Backside

I would say it's the hardest thing I ever went through in my life, for sure. But I would think that I probably learned more from it and probably am a different person in a positive way, I think, as a result of the divorce.

Kyle's divorce occurred 23 years ago. At that time, he had two children, a 15-year-old and a 13-year-old. Kyle did not know his wife was considering divorce; in his words, "it was a total surprise." His ex-wife abruptly left the marriage and their children.

> I had no indication, me or the kids, that she wasn't happy in the relationship. The shock was the biggest part. There was no conflict, there was no indication that she was unhappy in any way, so she just up and had her bags packed, said goodbye, and she was gone.

Kyle and his wife had participated in some marriage counseling; however, that experience was "horrible." Kyle does identify that his individual "divorce adjustment" counseling was "helpful" in his recovery. As with many who have a "bad" counseling experience, the experience itself has the potential to be more damaging to both the couple and individual than no counseling at all.

Kyle remained single for two years before marrying his current wife of 24 years. It was after marrying again that Kyle decided to pursue his career in counseling. Although Kyle was not a mental health professional at the time of his divorce, soon after his divorce, he created a support group for single parents at his church. He identifies that experience as "very rewarding" led him to considering a career in counseling. It would be about six years later that he would begin his new career as a mental health professional. Through his counseling training and work, he has also been able to identify some of his role contributing to the demise of his first marriage:

> And I had to do some changing on my side, too, because I had to be more domestic and do things that I probably—in retrospect—that I do now more in an equal kind of way with my wife, which I didn't back then. But I mean I didn't know any better and she [first wife] never told me any different so . . .

Our Stories

Barbara
Two Storms at Once

Would it help you to know if I'm married or not? And they both said, 'Yes, it would help us.' And I said, 'How would that help you?' They said . . . 'Because it shows us you are a human being.'

Barbara has been a mental health professional working with families and couples for the past 17 years. She has been married twice. Her first marriage lasted only a few years. From her first marriage, she and her ex-husband have one child. At the time of the divorce, her child was two years old. She married her second husband about four years later, and that marriage lasted about 12 years; she had no children from that marriage. Barbara has been single for about 11 years but is currently engaged.

Barbara felt that her divorce was "not conflictual," in fact they used the same divorce attorney and "agreed on absolutely everything." She shared that her husband "didn't want to get divorced. If I was okay with what he was doing [laugh] he would have been perfectly happy, but I wasn't and that was the problem, so it was really my decision."

Barbara felt her marriage had ended "a long time ago" before the decision to divorce. She felt this helped in feeling the decision was "right" and less painful:

> It was painful to cut that final string, but it was done and I knew that. The real work ahead of me was more to convince everyone else. Yes, he is wonderful in lots of ways. But you can't be married to someone who lives two different lives. If that's okay for you, then good. But I can't do that. So, I think that was what helped me too.

Barbara initially wanted to work on the marriage and had asked her husband to attend his own counseling as well as attend couples counseling. Unfortunately, the counseling proved fruitless. Just as

39

her husband had struggled with commitment to the relationship, her husband also lacked the commitment to change:

> I went and then found out that he was still doing the things he agreed not to do. In terms of couples counseling, when we went I thought we would be able to get over this but the more I learned as a counselor, the more I realized he has to want to make those changes for himself and do that himself and that I can't do this for him. It didn't matter how clean the house was or how good of a wife I was in any other way. How actualized I was becoming, how well the kids were cared for, none of that mattered. The piece that I was recognizing more and more was that it had nothing to do with me. It had to do with him and his choices.

Barbara was still working on saving her marriage even though her husband had moved out. However, only two weeks after her husband moved out of the house, she found a credit card statement with a bill from a dating service. That was the end.

Martin
Gone in 60 Seconds

And yet I guess the biggest thing for me is to know, to truly know, and I do know, all that has happened to me, including both divorces and other losses or experiences in my life, have made me part of who I am and part of how I can be helpful to other people.

Martin has been married twice. His first divorce occurred after 19 years of marriage. He and his first wife have two children from that marriage. For the interview, Martin chose to focus on the second marriage as he felt he had "resolved a lot about the first." His second divorce occurred three years ago after a brief marriage.

Martin believed when he married for the second time that "this would be it. I would grow old with this person and we would continue to grow closer and bond and see each other through the rest of our lives." He did feel they had some initial "struggles"; however, they "married anyway." Martin felt he did try to talk with his ex-wife; however, it was "not productive." In fact, he describes it as "hurtful and hard." She was only interested in an immediate divorce, so just six months from the day she left, the divorce was final. He went on to explain that:

> The issues began to get more pronounced and we went to counseling, but we would have really horrible arguments, screaming, acting in ways that I don't like acting. And her behavior scared me, she was extremely aggressive towards me and very angry and I responded either by being angry back or withdrawing. And of course, as I withdrew she got angrier, I'm sure, and so then she quit counseling with me in mid-April and then at the end of May that year she said she was leaving. And I didn't know that was going to happen and she was gone in 10 minutes. She had already packed through the week and I didn't realize that, and she had her car packed with the rest of the stuff. The dog was already in the car and she had the dog stuff and so truly in 10 minutes she was gone and we never reconciled.

I share with Martin the pain I see in his eyes even discussing the experience now. He acknowledges that the interview is "hard" but is willing to continue with the rest of the interview.

Martin had been a therapist for 30-plus years at the time of his second divorce. During the interview, he expressed feeling many emotions around the divorce; it was obvious that he is still impacted by the divorce from his second wife. Among those emotions there was "betrayal, abandonment, and loss." He also described feeling "shame, guilt, and embarrassment that I couldn't do it better." Martin continues to feel the embarrassment today as he provides not just counseling for couples, but also trainings for other therapists:

> It does, and comes up oftentimes in professional trainings, couples counseling trainings. I'm hearing and I'm teaching what are the right responses, what are the ways people can become closer and what they

need to stay in touch with and I just couldn't do it and she just couldn't do it. And it's embarrassing. And that comes up in my own practice with couples too. Because I'm teaching them also, helping them get closer and I know I didn't know how to do it for me.

Valerie
Devastated and Liberated

I don't feel much now. It's something that happened in my life that . . . Looking back it is kind of . . . I like where I am now, so if I didn't go through that, I wouldn't be where I am now. The experience as a whole gave more than it took.

Valerie was divorced 21 years ago after a nine-year marriage to her first husband. She had one child during that marriage who was seven years old at the time of the divorce. After being single for several years, she met her current husband and has been happily remarried for the past 14 years.

Valerie did try to work on her marriage and attended couples counseling until her husband decided he was ready to end the marriage:

I always held this wish that I could remain with the father of my child. So, it was kind of . . . I worked hard to keep my marriage together. But, my ex-husband had an affair, and that wasn't all it took for me to call it quits. I pursued help as long as he was willing to step in with me. And there was a point where I was literally devastated in the therapist office and he [ex-husband] said, 'I see her but I can't do anything about it.' And so, that's when I knew that we weren't going to be able to work on things. But, it took that for me to give up. So, I don't regret that. I feel like it was hard to that. But, I knew in order for me to be ok, I had to give this everything I could in order to allow myself to fully move on. So, it became liberating. I don't think it would have become liberating if I would not have been able to say, 'I'm going to do all I can before I walk away here.' And so, there was a lot of putting myself out there in a way that could result in nothing but humiliation, but I thought it was worth it, so I did it.

As mentioned previously, Valerie did meet with a couples counselor; however, she feels the approach/model utilized was not effective and her husband was not committed to the marriage:

Some of the models of course that we studied for working with couples were not out there at the time. That's not the kind of approach that therapists took with us. If it were, well, I'm just saying, I did not have the advantage of that. I had the advantage of somehow a quality of the work for me of you don't walk away from something this important any quicker than you absolutely have to. So, I never had many regrets because of that. Not much guilt because of that. It helped me tremendously. Being able to respect where I was to and not judge as much. Because there were certainly people who did judge. 'How could I work on a marriage where my husband had an affair?' or 'Was I crazy?' But, I'm sure there were times when I thought, 'I'm crazy.' But it really didn't take long before he really let me know he wasn't in it and he wasn't going to return to therapy. And I tried a little bit after that on my own. But I had to cut my losses and give more fully to myself and not 'us' anymore because he wasn't giving to us anymore.

Nick
A Blender of Emotions

So, it's been an education I would not undo this last six months for anything in the world because if I'm going to operate in life the way I want to I need to have balance of generosity and compassion, goodness, fallibility, and also, equally, how do I take care of myself.

Nick is currently in the process of finalizing his divorce. He has been married for almost 25 years and has two children out of the home and one teenage child who is still living in the home. He did seek marriage counseling prior to his separation. In fact, there were several counselors involved in the process who all worked collaboratively. The final outcome of the joint counseling was, "That dog don't hunt." In other words, the marriage was not going to survive.

Nick's wife had made the decision for the divorce and he felt he tried to make it easy for her and the children; however, there was a great deal of hostility surrounding his divorce:

> For the first few months it was upsetting but it felt necessary. And then after about 10 months, I started to realize that not only was I not being appreciated for the efforts I had been making. I had supplied all of the resources for the family and nothing had changed. But, I was getting consistent negative attitudes towards me and those parts of the marriage I had been at fault . . . for which I freely owned and for years I painfully apologized for. And, it felt like the separation was the correct path and I actually was happier than I have been in many years. So that part was a good experience and then it turned south where for me. I felt my ex was treating me . . . I felt very unjust.

Nick shared that after the lawyers became involved, the animosity became much worse: "And that got worse and worse and worse so initially it was like a three to like four or five in terms of animosity quality." Nick expressed feeling that it has been very helpful for him throughout the divorce process that he continues to have a solid relationship with his children:

> It's very, very strong and this hasn't really diminished that, other than I don't get to see them as much as I want to and share as much in their daily lives. We got our kids pretty much grown and it wasn't working and to continue would only be damaging all of us.

Nick is able to explore the pain he has been experiencing around the divorce: "The recent pain has been really about me and seeing my own self, and my failings and my vulnerabilities and my anxiety controlling me such that I have to remind myself to just have peace." In expanding on current his feelings surrounding his divorce, he describes a "blender of emotions":

> I have a mixture of relief, a sense of freedom and outrageous sadness . . . and a great deal of anger. Just a blender with all the emotions rolling

around, none of them seem to be absent. So, I have some affection for my life the way things went, some appreciation from what I learned from her, but some outrage that I put up with and couldn't see the mismatch, never honored the mismatch, saying, 'Wait a minute, this is this is why things are not working for me, is that you are not being the person I want you to be.' Now that doesn't mean she has to be; it means it's like me and Charlie Brown with a football: I keep not getting it.

Table 2.1 outlines major similarities and differences among the eight participants.

Table 2.1: Participant Summary

	Years Since Divorce	*Children in Home Time of Divorce*	*New Partner*	*Divorce Twice*	*Providing Counseling at Time of Divorce*	*Received Counseling*
Nick	0	1	NO	NO	YES	INDIVID/ COUPLE
Mary	9	3	NO	NO	YES	NO
Corey	10	0	YES	NO	NO	INDIVID
Catherine	4	1	YES	NO	YES	INDIVID/ COUPLE
Valerie	21	1	YES	NO	YES (STUDENT)	INDIVID/ COUPLE
Kyle	25	2	YES	NO	NO	INDIVID/ COUPLE
Barbara	27/11	1	YES	YES	YES	INDIVID/ COUPLE
Martin	25/3	2	NO	YES	YES	INDIVID

CHAPTER 3

EXPLORING PREVIOUS VIEWS OF DIVORCE: IMPACT OF OUR *FOO*

Our parents tell us to go out into the world and create our own families by committing to that *special someone*; they urge (beg) us to give them grandchildren and unfortunately often end up encouraging us to *stick with it* just as they have done. Bound by our family values and religious beliefs, we become confused and wounded when our relationships begin to falter; having no clear answers as to why the disconnect happened or how to reconcile and repair the damage. In these times, we might look to our families for comfort, or we might retreat to a place of shame and guilt.

Finding that forever partner, that *perfect match*, is made to look so easy. You can *Bumble it, Tinder it, Match it, Harmonize it* and even find that *special farmer* to date. In the Hollywood movies, there is a partner out there for each of us: our *one true love* who will meet every need and fill our souls with joy forever. Even the horror movies give a glimpse of romance when the hero saves the girl. In those iconic love stories, the lovers somehow magically know how to meet each other's needs, are always attuned with each other, and dream of *living happily ever after*. In the excitement of finding that *endless love* and deciding to commit to your life with a partner, the possibility of divorce seems unimaginable. The reality is that the complexity and convolutions of relationships often result in the love story becoming a tragic play.

As human beings we crave attachment and connections; we evolve best in systems. *FOO* is a phrase so common in the counseling world that we all know the meaning. Our *family of origin* is our first and most influential system. So, it's no surprise that the FOO can deeply color our personal view of marriage and divorce. For some, the thought of divorce may seem so foreign to reality that it shatters our identity and tattoos our foreheads with the label of failure. Depending on family history, religious beliefs, or culture, some have never experienced divorce. It may seem so totally foreign that it is truly an alien concept. What if we are shunned or rejected by our friends and community?

My *FOO* is complex in their beliefs and patterns. My families' religious faith tells us that marriage is a commitment *till death do you part*. You are expected to have more faith, pray more, be more submissive, and just not to give up. Above all, it is *best for the children*, so you just parents *hang in there*. And my parents did, despite years of turmoil and excruciating pain. I am sure the experience of seeing two people *hang in there* and be totally miserable somehow colored my reality of what a healthy relationship might look like. Did I enter into my own marriage with a mistrust that a healthy marriage is truly even possible? From that experience alone, am I more likely to encourage others to walk away and find their relief from the torture?

On the other side of the religious beliefs, is the reality of my extended family's history of divorce. In my family, divorce is almost a genetic trait that seems to be a part of our DNA; three generations of marriage fatalities that included grandparents, parents, various aunts, uncles, and cousins. At times, divorce seemed to be a long-awaited relief instead of a dreaded outcome. So, instead of viewing divorce as a failure, do I simply think of it as a developmental milestone?

As I now examine my own past and present beliefs surrounding divorce, I see a stark contrast between my childhood *FOO* experiences and my own divorce experience. I am flooded with childhood memories: verbally violent arguments; abrupt midnight awakenings as my mother grabs me out of the bed to leave the house; years of excuses, forgiveness, and perseverance. In my family, there is no shame in divorce. In fact, in some ways it feels more shameful to have never taken the leap into marriage than to announce an upcoming divorce.

And yet, my own divorce, remarriage, and divorce was so quiet that many of our friends didn't even notice. In fact, when we divorced the second time, most of our friends thought it was the first. As many couples do, we kept trying to make our children happy by *staying a family*. Yet, there were years of pain and conflict that only our children witnessed. There was never any thought of couples counseling (both times) because it would be too painful to actually say out loud the deep fear that the marriage just could not work. I am certain that divorce was an acceptable option to me, but because I wanted to keep my children happy, I felt an obligation to stay in the marriage till the bitter end, almost feeling like the captain of a sinking ship.

How does this shape my work as a couples therapist? I honestly had not considered any of these questions until I began my research. I knew that my goal was to always *bracket out* my own values and beliefs, but I had not taken the time to sit back and thoroughly explore that my own divorce experience might have changed my beliefs or attitude towards marriage and how I approach counseling.

In Catherine's family of origin, divorce was very accepted. Her grandparents were divorced, her father had been previously married before he married her mother and they were divorced after 30 years of marriage. Catherine's views have not necessarily changed but have "expanded." Although the painful marriage has ended, her ex-husband continues to inflict pain in a different way. He has continued to bring her to court for issues surrounding her children, so Catherine's experience has illuminated a new possibility that she had not previously considered: the painful possibility that divorce is not always a "final detachment."

Nick did not have any strong deterrents from his family of origin surrounding divorce. There were no particular religious beliefs passed down that impacted his feelings around divorce:

Well, probably the opposite of what most people say: My religious beliefs are that it's okay to divorce. My religious beliefs are that two people are to be following their personal truths. And can they appreciate the others' truths and then find a transcended reality together. Like okay, 'I can accommodate to this'; kind of like, 'You like Brussels sprouts; I don't like Brussels sprouts. I can make them for you but not me.' We can find a way to accommodate each other's world without being illegal or somehow God is judging us kind of thing. I don't think God works that way or whatever God is. So, the religious beliefs are that there is the right to pursue freedom and happiness as long as you are being responsible. And you shouldn't be controlled by a Catholic church, or you shouldn't be controlled by a community that says, 'No, we need you to stay married,' or parents who say 'No, divorce is terrible. Suffer like the rest of us.' Any of that kind of ethical, moral crap that people throw through the lens of religion, I don't believe in that.

Divorce was viewed as "a tragedy but often necessary." Nick describes his family history in a unique way:

It wasn't viewed moralistically. But I have a weird family when it comes to things [laugh]. My family is chock full of affairs. So, there's this kind of release from the Christianity of it all. And, so divorce is seen as just one of the 'Well, I broke my arm' kind of thing. Or, 'That's what you have to go through.'

For Valerie, the divorce process itself was "sad, adversarial, and liberating." However, she remembers that as "devastating" as it was, "I don't recall ever really feeling or being, maybe I felt it, but completely alone." Valerie identifies her family as supporting her:

So, I had family, that . . . At least when I'm hurting the most, family has my back. When I don't look like I'm hurting enough, when I don' t look like I'm sacrificing, it's harder for family to have my back. But when I was hurting the most—so I really didn't have to avoid my pain to much. So that made it easier to feel it. Because it was okay. People were not going to leave me because I was hurting. So, I felt abandoned by him, but not so much ... It doesn't mean I have a perfect family but, when you're hurting the most, that's when they are most comfortable stepping up. They struggle more to celebrate with you. They are able to be in your pain a little bit more.

Both of Valerie's parents were from families that "didn't get divorced"; however, they themselves had divorced because of reasons similar to those of Valerie and her husband. Her father grew up in a "strong, Catholic, conservative, Italian" family:

> I guess somehow these beliefs are stronger from my dad. But it was instilled in me probably because of his strong Catholic faith, dedication, and family beliefs and values. But he instilled in me that you learn everything you can, you work as hard as you can, but, ultimately, you have to make sure you're okay and as much as a marriage should provide that for you. It may not. So, I just remember times before when I would talk to my dad about my ex-husband and what was going on with us to some degree. Because he could be there. If I was sacrificing and hurting so, it was easy to talk to my dad about how I was hurting. He would try to help me see how marriages are just tough and I'm going to need to stick it out and work through it. But then, ultimately, when he knew that what the circumstances were and he knew how much I was still trying, he respected that. He respected me where I was and that I needed to do what I needed to do.

Valerie's father was raised in the Catholic church, and she felt that had an influence on her in when she was experiencing her divorce:

> I guess even though I come from my dad's strong Catholic background—all of my dad's family, who I am very, very close with—somehow the shame didn't stay with me very long. You know, but he did, he had other ways of letting me know I wasn't doing the right thing. But he was ... it actually brought me close to him. And if that could have, that could have—I could have been so scared to get divorced because it

could have ostracized me from the family. That's not what happened. I really didn't have that.

Despite having a Catholic family background, Valerie feels she does not bring any particular faith into her counseling relationships:

I'm so interested in learning their beliefs, a little bit more of seeing the value in all faiths or kind of world religions. So, I can be completely invested in one and dedicated to one and see value in another. And I also kind of dedicate myself to what I see in all faiths, which is the acceptance of love for the struggles and the challenges of all relationships. And that some relationships come to end and that you're not judged for that or you are not . . . And maybe that was in me when I kept fighting for it or kept stepping up for it. But then was also able to let go of it. And I didn't feel like it, not even my strict Catholic extended family, they still loved me. And even now they don't see me as probably as strong of a Catholic because I've really got more of a balanced faith through my mother as well.

Mary shared that, in her family, "people just don't get divorced." Her mother was against her divorce and she had "a very hard time accepting it." However, in listening to Mary's story, it seemed as that by the time the decision to divorce had been made, she was very much at peace with the decision:

I think for me before I decided to get a divorce . . . that was the time I processed. Like I processed everything prior to the actual divorce. I think for some people divorce is a process in itself. Like they decide to get divorced and then they go through everything. I went through everything and so when I decided to get divorced, I had already made the decision and we both . . . it was just a matter of completing the paperwork and getting it done. So, I had already processed it.

In Corey's family of origin, divorce is "viewed negatively"; however, "just about everyone has had one." Corey shared that his feelings of shame around the divorce were not directly from his family; however, he did connect it back to that:

> I felt a lot of shame about it, but that is probably related to my family of origin. In kind of my own sense of needing to get it right. But I don't think it was directly related to the context of divorce or to that . . . I think it was more to do with my own desire and need to be performing and getting things right, being 'perfect.' I'm aware that's impossible, but . . . [laugh] I think they were pretty supportive for the most part. In the end, they kind of said 'What are you doing, get divorced already.' I mean it was three years of her kind of being gone so . . .

Martin describes his parents as "very Italian." He said divorce was "not mentioned" and, in fact, he "never heard that word." He expressed feeling that it was "hard" for his parents to see him get a divorce. For him, this also brought feelings of shame: "I felt shame there too. Again, being a therapist and getting divorced." In discussing his own religious beliefs surrounding divorce, he views things a bit different from how his family and his religious faith do:

> In general, I do think that God gives us an opportunity to heal in marriages; I really do believe that. And so, I try to sometimes introduce that or foster the idea, if they introduce it to me, that that is true. But I also believe there are times when a marriage has died, it's done, and it's right to leave that marriage. So, I think God brings many couples to heal and see life through forever, and I think maybe God brings some couples together to do some kind of work for a certain amount of time, and then when that time is done, it's done. And I guess that's the truth. Because even if it's a horrible thing, it's an opportunity for growth that God presents. So, I see it from that spiritual perspective.

In Barbara's family of origin, divorce was "not acceptable." When she called her mother, distraught over finding the dating service information, her mother still encouraged her to continue working on the marriage. Barbara was very affected by her mother's lack of support:

> She [my mother] apologized but it took us awhile to just kind of get back to our normal relationship. I pulled back, so I felt like I lost not just my second husband, who was a good stepdad, but I also felt like I lost my parents somewhat.

Having already experienced one divorce, Barbara expressed feeling a deeper impact by her second divorce:

> So, it was painful because I already felt like a failure because of my first marriage. Being raised Catholic and Polish, it's like 'that's it, you stick with it and you get through it.' So, it was very painful . . . And so I was raised to stay with the marriage and I really did think that this was going to be it. It was really painful because we were married for 12 years when we divorced but had not really separated at all during that time. The identity of being married, the stability of being married—so there were a lot of subsequent losses that went along with that.

Barbara frequently mentioned her families' ethnic and religious background as influencing her feelings around divorce prior to her own experience:

> Polish, Catholic, I mean there is no such word [divorce] right? You just suck it up and deal with it. You are supposed to do it and it doesn't matter if the other person is going against whatever agreement you made in terms of your expectations for the relationship. In growing up, I had one aunt who was divorced very late in life. She was shunned for it. The deal was what do you need to do to keep the marriage together even it means stick your head in the sand or as in, 'You know what is going on and pretend you don't,' or 'Don't even try to look around just try to

Exploring Previous Views of Divorce

create your own sanctuary.' I think that's pretty much . . . Divorce was just not acceptable.

Kyle's family was "supportive" and "comforting" around his divorce. They were aware he did not have a choice in the decision:

> It was a horrible thing and they didn't see it, but it wasn't like a spiritual issue of any kind. They were hurting for me as parents would, but I don't think it . . . And they were very comforting during that time. They never gave their opinions and, well, I didn't have a choice, that decision was already made way before she said goodbye. My family was very supportive, but the religious system I was working within was not.

At the time of his divorce, Kyle had dedicated six years of his life working with a missionary organization in "dangerous foreign countries." The response by his organization was confusing for him and had a long-term significant impact:

> I was a missionary at the time and one of the things I really loved doing was going to summer camps and stuff and showing slides from my work; I liked doing that with kids. But, they called and said that I was divorcing and could no longer do that because I was divorced—that disqualified me from doing that—this was very confusing for me. It's the opposite of wanting to support me or check on me. The only conversation was to inform me that I could not do that work anymore. I wasn't all that surprised by it, but it was very devastating to me. This person [ex-wife] decided to no longer have a life with me and our kids, and now I am somehow less than and disqualified. It didn't add up. The reality it is that it is unavoidable at times. Yes, it cost me. Like anything else, we may have a *head knowledge* of what we believe until we are faced with life real situations.

The response from his organization to his divorce not only changed his professional path, it had an impact on his spiritual path. This change would be intertwined in his next career and his work with couples as a mental health professional. Kyle's feeling was that:

> If they [the religious organization] wanted to look at it from a religious perspective, I think it didn't add up. It helped me actually because I realized how it just didn't make sense. It caused me to reevaluate my belief systems and decide what I do believe and what I don't believe and what's the difference between spirituality and religion. How easy it is to confuse the two. It added a 'more deeper' spiritual faith that was less defined by rules and regulations.

Kyle's pain from his divorce experience further changed his previous feelings around divorce as well as his understanding of client behaviors.

> I think before you have experienced the level of pain that divorce brings you, it's easy to say, 'Well there's a right and a wrong.' It's like dualistic thinking; there's a right and a wrong. But after you have experienced that pain and gone through that experience, it changes how you see things. You see that things aren't so right and wrong, not so black and white. And it's less about sin. That was a big shift for me, it moved it from being categorized as right and wrong, sin and good; it was just pain. I think almost every behavior I see underneath it is understandable if we can sit with it long enough to figure it out. I think that was shaped by my painful experience of divorce. I think that was what changed my mind, that painful experience of divorce. It helps with understanding.

Kyle shared that although his religious beliefs had somewhat changed since the divorce, he remains a Christian. In his work with clients, when he "brings God into the room, it's what's going on with me; it's not an expectation of what's going on with them." He explained that he doesn't bring up praying in a session, "but I might be praying my way through the whole session. But they don't know that."

CHAPTER 4

WORKING ON SELF-AWARENESS AND RECOVERY

"I'm so sorry," is often the expression offered when we share the news of a divorce. There's the assumption that something painful or traumatic has occurred and we should offer our condolences. When a relationship ends, does it feel like we are hemorrhaging from our soul? Is there an expectation for me to heal quickly before the hemorrhaging stops? Diving deep into the layers and *parts of self* that become impacted with the loss of a relationship requires time and introspection. As mental health professionals do we know all of the questions we should ask and answer for ourselves as we recover from the life crisis of divorce? The barrage of questions we should explore, hitting us below the belt and adding to an already unbalanced state, include:

Am I able to recognize if I am still in crisis? If I am still experiencing pain and grief from the loss, is it affecting how I work with my couples? Do my clients notice any subtle changes? Is it possible that I am covering up the pain with anger? Am I aware of times I might be getting angry with one of the partners because it's touching on my pain? How attuned am I to my own feelings? Can I see if my wounds are still raw or have started to heal? Am I gaining insight from my own mistakes? As time passes, do I have enlightenment as to what went wrong in my marriage? If I watched my children in pain and grief, totally damaged from the tornado of my divorce, do I think it's wiser to convince couples to stay together to protect their children? Is there a part of a me that moves more into a role of psycho-educator in order to teach clients lessons based on my own divorce experiences and not what is actually going on with the client? Do I still have many bleeding wounds or feelings of resentment that cloud my ability to meet the needs of my clients? How do I feel when asked by clients for wisdom and guidance? Am I fully aware if there is any lingering pain or emotion attached to my responses? Do I jump at the chance to enlighten, or am I able to sit back and process my clients' issue and not my own?

It is vital that therapists not allow their own personal values and beliefs to impact interactions during counseling (Kocet & Herlihy, 2014; Pope & Vasquez, 2011). As a mental health professional, there exists an obligation for the therapist to avoid inflicting any harm to the client. This requires a constant focus on self-awareness and identification of personal biases in order to maintain a professional and therapeutic relationship with clients.

Due to the unique quality of the therapeutic relationship, any interference in a therapist's personal life has a potential impact on the therapeutic relationship. When therapists experience their own mental or physical stressor, a decision must be made as to if a respite is needed and what that might entail. Self-awareness is crucial at this time in order to avoid potential blocks and countertransference issues that might arise from the mental health professional returning to work prior to processing their own personal crisis issues (Counselman & Alonso, 1993).

Previous research has focused on the necessity of the clinician to focus on attending to their own issues and needs in order to provide effective therapy to clients (Gelso & Hayes, 2007; Rønnestad & Skovholt, 2012; Skovholt & Jennings, 2004). Undeniably, every life experience impacts all of us (Aponte & Kissil, 2014; Baldwin, 2000; Gerson, 1996). The experience of divorce is no different. Participants in my research identified self-awareness as the most valuable element to recovery from divorce and subsequently being able to effectively work with clients. When clinicians were able to receive either their own supportive counseling or counseling education (that was specific to relationships), they reported a gain of insight that improved their awareness in their roles in relationships and in providing therapy.

Even in the best of circumstances, recovery from any life crisis such as divorce can take time. There is a process to grieving the loss of any relationship. As mental health professionals, we routinely encourage and advise clients to "take time to recover." We assure them that there will be unexpected times when the emotions surrounding a painful or traumatic event will just *pop up* and surprise them. We might even give them tools to use when (not if) they are thrown off by the immersion of the emotion. Do we have those tools in our own tool kits? Are we aware and honest with ourselves that we might fall victim to being blindsided during a session?

As with any human event or crisis, working with couples in distress might trigger many of the therapists' own wounds from their personal relationships. Once triggered, the emotional reaction has the potential to impact the therapist's ability to counsel from a place of neutrality. Maintaining this neutrality requires therapists to be persistent in examining their own feelings and biases. Therapists have a duty to be attuned and vigilant in identifying when their own personal issues impact their work with clients (Aponte & Carlson, 2009; Aponte & Kissil, 2014; Cheon & Murphy, 2007).

Since the time of Sigmund Freud, those providing counseling to others have been encouraged to undergo their own analysis in order to achieve more self-awareness. Others, such as Murray Bowen, Mary Ainsworth, and Virginia Satir, focused on exploration of attachments and differentiation from the family of origin in order to examine issues that might interfere with a clinicians' work with clients (Satir, 2000; Skowron & Dendy, 2004). According to Nelson et al. (1993), utilization of the *self-of-the-therapist* skills is vital in providing effective and non-judgmental counseling. The more in-depth the clinicians' self-awareness, the more skilled they become in identifying their own challenges in therapeutic work with clients. Sharma and Fowler (2016) suggest that in order for counselors to remain attuned and present in the therapeutic process, the therapist must participate in ongoing self-awareness.

Although not all of those interviewed participated in personal counseling, all participants expressed that continuing to learn through counseling training and workshops was a motivating force in pushing them to examine, process, and heal. The participants expressed feeling that the knowledge provided them with a clearer understanding of their own role in their previous relationship. Working on the *person-of-the-therapist* was crucial in their goal to maintain an awareness of how their experiences might influence their relationships and work with clients.

Similar to a few of the participants, I am more cognizant of my emotions surrounding my marriage and divorce during the times I am involved in trainings and workshops with colleagues. I believe it is during these times that I am more attuned to my own *person-of-the-therapist* work, which illuminates my own mistakes and role in my failed marriage. My goal when working with clients is to focus is on *being present* and *in the room,* in order to gain understanding of the human beings that have trusted me to work with them. However, I am aware that it is my responsibility to always be examining and evaluating the impact of the tsunamis and hurricanes in life that put my therapeutic balance at risk.

I am mindful to honor my clients for taking the time and energy (both emotional and physical) to participate in counseling. I have heard countless stories from clients who are disheartened and discouraged from years of meeting with therapists and still feeling lost and confused. Clients who knew the names of the therapist's children and enjoyed the weekly discussions of the latest news or sports, without feeling they had achieved any personal growth, enlightenment, or resolution. Some clients who actually *wanted* to talk about the constant conflict, the deep pain and trauma of an experience, but were advised by their therapist to focus on the positives in their relationships and

Working on Self-Awareness and Recovery

identify skills that would encourage better communication and "better ways to manage the joint checkbook" (true story). In my research, I explored how therapists, who might be wounded and scared from their own divorce, have been working to achieve self-awareness in order to avoid any impact the experience might have on their work.

Personally, I did not meet with a counselor until years after my second divorce (despite the constant requests from my children). Although I was quite committed to the idea of reaching to others for advice and wisdom, I preferred the more casual approach. I frequently had long conversations with my friends and colleagues, who patiently and gently supported me. There was the occasional push to examine how my *assertiveness* and *pursuing* might have played a role in an event. But, for the most part, there was just thoughtful validation and empathy (which of course felt wonderful). I was fully aware that I was avoiding a deep exploration experience that would open that Pandora's Box of pain; that experience of saying something out loud that makes it more real and heartbreaking. So, in the end, I definitely benefited from my personal counseling experience. My therapist challenged me to explore feelings and behaviors that I needed to change. It wasn't always pleasant, but it was always fruitful. And it did enlighten me to areas in my past and in my own belief system that might color my work with my clients.

I was working on my counseling education between my first divorce and remarriage (to the same man), so, initially, my own divorce experience did not impact my counseling work. During my internships, I worked in the counseling office of a local university, so I very rarely met with a couple. It was not until I began my training in Emotionally Focused Therapy that the wounds were ripped open and the real risks became apparent. I literally was in training to learn every detail of how to be an effective counselor with couples, as I was in the process of ending my own marriage (for the second time). And, instead of taking time off, I shifted from working with university students to opening a private practice and working with couples; I joined the ranks of those who distract instead of deal.

As my training progressed and we were forced to examine and discuss our own relationships, I become more cognizant of how my past relationship struggles could impact my work with clients. I could see where I might be more inclined to validate and empathize with the Pursuer and to be frustrated with the *frozenness* of the Withdrawer. Through the role plays and enactments, I also became acutely aware of how it felt to sit in the chair of the Withdrawer: not really knowing what to say, so not saying anything at all. The Withdrawer, who is always trying to sit on the land mine to keep it from exploding.

In the beginning of my training, I clearly remember working with a couple and feeling that I was being equally empathetic and compassionate to both. I remember being proud of my validation skills and how I balanced the time given to each partner in sharing their story. My awareness of this misperception was made clear when the Withdrawer stood up, shared her feeling that I had totally missed how she felt about the issues in the relationship and then left the session. In reviewing my work with the couple, I realized I had been validating the Pursuer for his commitment in *working so hard in session*, but not validating that it was just as hard for the Withdrawer to just show up to a session and listen without really knowing how to respond.

For many years, Catherine attended marriage counseling with her ex-husband. Unfortunately, when looking back, she is now aware that the experience was not beneficial in providing her with insight into the working on the relationship. She has a new awareness that the approach utilized by her therapist might have just put a Band-Aid on the situation and not aided in resolving any issues:

> Having an old-school therapist in that role, she [the therapist] became one of my attachments, which could have been a problem, and when I look back I think that was very possibly a problem in my marriage— that I was probably more attached to her [the marriage therapist]. But she, as a psychologist, was also treating him and she understood the very difficult personality aspect of it. So, she probably kept us married

longer, if I had to guess. Because we would go in to see her and it was sort of like a pressure cooker valve. I look at the therapy and don't think that was particularly helpful. In terms of actually bonding us to one another. I absolutely see that as an issue.

Catherine was never able to take a break to recover from the trauma of her divorce, partly because her ex-husband has continued to be on the attack, and partly because she could not financially afford to take any time off. As with several of the participants, Catherine was not meeting with couples at the time of her divorce:

> Fortunately, I wasn't seeing couples at that point; I was just doing individual therapy. I had not gotten into doing couples. So, there was no need to take a break. I had to continue to work, I was being . . . I really didn't have a choice on that because I was bleeding financially with legal fees.

For the past three years, Catherine has expanded her own training to include a more attachment-based approach. The model forces Catherine to look inward and examine her own relationships and roles she participated in that have contributed to the disconnect. Catherine truly feels this new insight has opened doors for her and impacted her ability to be more self-aware of her current reactions with her ex-husband:

> A few years after my divorce, I started studying an attachment-based model and it really helped me organize it in a very different way. My own participation in my first marriage, and that I would experience things and think things that I wouldn't share. And what that was like. I think I've become much 'more clear' about the different roles [with her ex-husband]. When he starts to really get frenzied I may go the attachment model. The model gives me a framework to see this in. That he [her ex-husband] becomes frenzied for whatever reason. Sometimes it may have something to do with me and sometimes it doesn't have

anything to do with me. If one of the children pulls away from him, then he'll come back and start pulling stuff with me. He and I do not have a . . . We are very cordial, we can be in the same room, it's fine.

Catherine feels she is able to utilize this new awareness when helping her clients understand their own reactions to their partners when they get stuck in their cycles.

As mentioned earlier, Kyle and his wife had participated in some marriage counseling; however, that experience "actually made matters worse."

> I was devastated. I remember the only word the guy told me was that I was 'co-dependent' and she was something . . . I forgot. He labeled both of us as we were going out the door. I didn't think he had a clue. So, I was hurt because I loved her not because there was something wrong with me [laugh]. That was confusing to me. So that was a very negative experience, which I think, in some ways, I mean looking back on it, I think in some ways that probably helped me to really want to do a good job as a counselor. I knew what it was like if you didn't do a good job as a counselor.

Similar to Catherine, Kyle feels that he gains awareness by working with a therapeutic model that demands the clinician be present and "in the room" with clients. Kyle not only utilizes the model but he trains others in the model, so he is aware of the impact he has not only on clients, but on the therapists he trains and their clients.

Barbara's divorce occurred as her family was recovering from the effects of Hurricane Katrina. Barbara did continue with her own counseling during the divorce process; "I was in counseling in a very specialized group for therapists. There was a counselor leading the group and it was all counselors in the group." She describes this group counseling as "one of the most wonderful experiences of my life." She added that:

The personal counseling was pivotal for me . . . In helping to heal and find the courage to initiate the divorce process. I really don't know if I could have done it. Yes, really pivotal for me in terms of finding the courage because I didn't have a network of people who were accepting of divorce other than my group and co-workers.

Barbara was living in a trailer in her driveway while repairs were being done to her family home. It was her co-workers who had helped her gut her home after it had been flooded in the hurricane. With the additional support from her co-workers, Barbara did not feel she needed to take a break from her work with clients. In fact, Barbara felt that her work "definitely" helped her get through the divorce.

I had started working with them in 2001 and was close with all these people and we talked about all of our own issues too. Not just our family lives but our own issue and how our client issues were impacting us. So, I had so much support, I didn't, actually the thought never even occurred to me to take a break; I didn't need to. I will say I can remember sitting . . . we all sat in the same places and we would all bring food, so it was like a pot luck every week and we would sit and eat and I can remember thinking . . . 'So, I need to tell everybody that this is what I am going through but how do I do this without bursting out into tears?' And of course, I couldn't. As soon as I said it I was choking up and getting all teary and I didn't want to look at anybody because I knew as soon as I looked at them they would be able to see my pain and they would feel it too. So, but I mean they rallied around me.

Barbara did take time off from her work because the hurricane had damaged her daughter's school, so she needed to be home to take care of her. During that time, her boss frequently called her to return to work: "We need you and you need to be back at work." Barbara was aware of the potential impact of her own crisis situation and expressed concerns with her ability to help clients. Her supervisor had a different perspective of how Barbara's own life crisis might impact her work with clients:

> After Katrina, my supervisor was handing cases out and she gave me a couple of cases and I remember saying to her, 'How am I going to help these people? Their life is such a mess?' And she said to me, 'You are the only one that can help this family because you are the only one living in a camper and having to deal with losing your home and have your husband living in another state somewhere.' And I know she was just being a cheerleader but she was right in that adversity does make us better counselors. I was better at that time in helping those families than I would have been previously.

Nick was in the midst of his divorce when I interviewed him and I wondered how this pain might currently be impacting him and if he had taken some time off from working with clients. He shared that he had taken a break, but it had been due to a physical injury from an accident and not his divorce:

> So, on one hand, I did have a sense of relief; okay, I did have a break, I need just to settle down and come to terms with this and mourn the loss of this life that I thought I was living and no longer is available. So, taking a break was helpful but I wasn't inclined to say, 'Oh, I need a break because I'm going through a divorce.' I didn't give myself that sort of opportunity. I wanted to tough it out and I also felt that in some ways it would be a helpful distraction.

Corey feels he has benefited from his own personal counseling in addition to his current training in an attachment-based model. He is active in trainings and workshops that help him focus on *person-of-the-therapist*.

Corey's final comments focus on awareness and the importance of utilizing techniques and skills that improve awareness in your counseling work. "I guess awareness is the big key." He identifies that

WORKING ON SELF-AWARENESS AND RECOVERY

awareness is necessary at a cognitive, emotional, and physical level. "Like if my body kind of speeds up or my tone or pace kind of speeds up I have to be aware of that. But it really doesn't happen that much anymore because I think of the processing that I have done in the past, but yeah. I had to process it." Initially, Corey had only processed his divorce with friends, so he felt it was not "organized" and did not "make sense" yet:

> And to go on and organize it with somebody kind of making sense of the story I think helped. If you don't know you been through something or if you haven't worked through it, those are the important parts. It will definitely affect you; you don't know what's happening, so, as far as divorce and your counseling practice. I think have an awareness around it and working through this stuff with somebody—if not somebody, at least programs. I mean there are a lot of places that you can go to kind of process your story.

Corey identified utilizing friends, his counseling program, supervisors, and colleagues to process his story. His advice is to "Go work through it if you have had the experience." He is aware that after the passage of 10 years, he feels different about his divorce experience: "So just as my perspective has changed with time and life and relationships . . . also the ability to look at myself and that whole cycle and system."

In light of the fact that Corey works in a faith-based community, I wondered if he had an awareness of how this population might impact the interventions he utilizes in in his work:

> I don't think it has an affect on my interventions necessarily. I think being aware of all people's faith . . . I try to take everyone's spiritual beliefs into account and so then me having my own [belief] and disclosing it is really beneficial in that sense. I say beneficial; I mean I don't even push it and sometimes faith doesn't even come up. Except for in my intake, I do have a question that talks about spirituality and the inclusion of it in our discussions. But other than that, I really let the client lead that. I try to stay out of the ditch of with my counseling

67

private practice. I incorporate a faith aspect if asked but basically an Emotionally Focused Therapy (EFT) perspective. I'm trained in Solution Focused, Cognitive Behavioral Therapy (CBT), and Motivational Interviewing, but always from EFT frame.

Valerie was just returning to school when her marriage started to struggle. For her, school was actually a "distraction" from her pain. There was no space for recovery time from her "turbulence." She was aware that her marriage was flailing, but she did not have the option of taking a break from the pursuit of her career.

> And I went thru some pretty deep pain. And, it was starting to show up, some of the marital issues, were starting to show up prior to me going back to school and then it started to shift more and more. And that focus of doing something that big for myself helped me to not be so overwhelmed by it. But I was still feeling a lot of inner turbulence. It was distraction, but it also was the School of Social Work, I knew it would help you to be in your stuff. For me it did because I was a little bit older student. I was 27–28 first time being in graduate school.
>
> So, it was just . . . I had thought "I can't go back to school now," so I took one class because I wanted to be in school, but I can't because I'm too busy and I have a child and I was concerned about my marriage a little bit then. It wasn't as big, but it got bigger. But, yes I kind of feel like it helped me to understand a little more of what I was . . . It kept me busy too, but it wasn't studying something so far removed. It was about relationships so . . . It was . . . It gave me a healthy focus so that I wasn't overwhelmed and consumed totally by the heartache.

Valerie felt she could not put off finishing school or working with clients in her internship because she had to create a new life and support herself and her daughter:

> I didn't really have a way of providing for myself so that was the scariest part of the divorce. How am I going to do this? So work was very

Working on Self-Awareness and Recovery

exciting, fulfilling and liberating because I am getting to that place that this will never happen again. And I was getting to it pretty quick so that was good.

In her first job after graduation, Valerie was expected to work with more couples. She realized that there was the potential for her divorce to impact her work with clients, and she asked for a break:

> Then when I graduated I was doing more couples. And the divorce was still very fresh, so did I feel to take a break? I 'm not remembering having so many couples at that time. But I do remember kind of being given a heavier case load than others. It was just thought by my supervisor that 'Valerie can handle this.' Probably because I put off an air that I could handle it. But it was a lot; it was a lot. And I do remember talking to my supervisor saying 'You know this is—I love the work, it's not because I don't want to do it, it's because I feel like I may not be able to do my best. I'm sure I'm not doing my best because I'm dealing with some of my own stuff.'

As I observe Martin sharing his story, I see the pain in his eyes as he recounts the experience. He acknowledges that the interview is "hard" but chooses to continue with the rest of the interview. Martin initially did not take a break from his work in counseling couples; however, as he participated in more of his own professional training in working with couples, he did decide to take a step back:

> I realized that, 'I just can't do this right now; it's too painful.' I'm too much in touch with my own wounding and again the ways that I responded. And too much in pain about how her wounds wounded me, the way she treated me. And so, I just couldn't do that and so I found what I did was that when a couple would call, I would just say I didn't have an opening, and I would refer them out to people that I trusted. Just found ways to say that 'I'm not available,' and the couples that I already had, I hung in there with. I hope I was good enough for them

during that time. But, no, and I still haven't fully opened the door to couples. I'm very selective and still haven't opened up enough to couples. I think there is still some healing I have to do I think. But I think I'm at that place where I can begin to do it and do it in a more inner peaceful way. But it's still hard.

In recanting the story of her marriage conflict and ultimate divorce, Mary seems very "matter of fact" with the details. There was definitely a *tone* and *feel* during her interview that was different from the others. There is a sense of calm and peace with no apparent signs of pain or anger in discussing the experience. She expressed feeling that by the time of her divorce, all of the emotions and pain had really subsided.

Although Mary was able to continue her work during the *challenging* times in her marriage, I did wonder if Mary's clients might have noticed any changes in their work together during that period—subtle changes that she might not have perceived. If a client doesn't bring this to our attention, how would we know? As human beings, can we really mask all of our own trials and tribulations in order to keep them out of the counseling session? Do we take a risk by not exploring and processing our own life crises with our own mental health professional?

CHAPTER 5

IS MY OWN "STUFF" GETTING IN THE WAY?

Therapeutic Skills 101 addresses the issue of countertransference. If the characters and the plot feel like I am watching a Hallmark movie of my life, can I be fair? Even Freud addressed the issue of countertransference. From a psychoanalytic perspective, the therapist refrains from self-disclosure in order to promote transference from the client to the therapist. The therapist can utilize countertransference as a tool for examining characteristics of the client that might be impacting relationships outside of the therapeutic relationship.

Additionally, the therapist must examine what thoughts and feelings are being triggered by the client but are not attributable to the client. The real question is, am I aware when issues of countertransference arise? Do I find myself attracted to or repulsed by a client for reasons I am not able to identify? As a human being dealing with the crisis of divorce, am I able to simultaneously be an effective therapist supporting clients in a marriage that is crumbling?

Human emotions play a crucial role in the perceived experience of the event and how they respond to later triggers around the event. Clinicians who are still angry or in pain from their own divorce experience might avoid working with certain clients or might struggle with being neutral when working with couples. Furthermore, clinicians still in crisis and fragile from their own divorce might be at an increased risk for inappropriate self-disclosure, countertransference, and ineffective therapeutic interventions. If therapists are currently in a happy second marriage or new relationship, will they be more willing to guide an unhappy couple towards ending the relationship for a potentially more successful union?

Most participants noticed that at times a client has shared a story that resembled their own relationship struggles. As human beings, we tend to move in similar patterns and cycles, so it's not surprising that our own story has parallels to others'. Some of the participants noticed that when the similarities highlighted previous personal mistakes made, it forced them to be more mindful of any reaction they might experience during a session. Others felt confident they were not impacted by clients who shared relationship struggles that were similar to theirs.

Kyle had been divorced for a few years before he began his counseling career and did not feel that hearing a story similar to his own was particularly triggering for him.

> I don't think so. I'm trying to be honest. I think again because I know how we survived it and all came out better and very close. I probably have a relationship with my kids now that I would not have had outside of that.

Occasionally, I have noticed times when the couple shared a story very similar to mine and I find myself "stepping out of the present" and noticing a twinge of discomfort; being in a session when you feel as though the universe has a sense of humor and has brought a "mirror couple" onto your office:

> Johnny and Maggie were really struggling to stay in their marriage. They have been together for 28 years, raised three children, and had a successful business together. They had been "happy enough" over the years and were both committed to "keeping the family together." But now that the children were grown and out of the house, they were

realizing that did not have much in common, and in fact, they did not like each other very much. They lived in together in the same home, but more like roommates than a married couple.

As I listened to their story, I couldn't help but feel the parallel to my life. At times, I felt I knew what they would say even before they spoke the words. In the process of my research, I began to explore the impact of my *old stuff* and how that might have influenced my work with clients. During sessions, I hear my own voice: "I remember feeling that way," "I know exactly what you mean!" Did I subconsciously protect the partner I identified with? Was I empathetic enough with the partner who "pushed that button"? Can I distance myself enough to not be activated? As an EFT therapist, I am trained to "be present" with my clients and "lean in" to the emotions in the room. What do I do if the emotion that comes up for me is negatively affecting my ability to work with a client? Am I ashamed of something I did (or didn't do) in my marriage, and does that come up for me when my client expresses a similar situation? Am I blinded to other things that I can't see? To the man that only has a hammer is everything a nail?

I am acutely aware of the fact that I was not able to share that vulnerable place with my partner. As I work with couples, trying to convince them to have the courage the strip away the protective armor and take the risk to go to that place, I know their bodies respond with fear and doubt. I remember my own body's response when considering the risk of opening up to discuss the loneliness and sadness I felt in our relationship. In sessions, I am continually checking myself, "Do you feel tense? Are you clenching your teeth? Are you leaning in and open? Are you in some way uncomfortable with what your client is sharing?" I believe it is impossible for me to be attuned to my client, to be fully present and engaged, and not in some way be impacted by the story they are sharing. Accepting this as truth opens the door to removing issues with *resistant* clients due the potential *blocks* brought in the therapists' own stuff.

Inadvertently, pain frequently befalls intimate relationships. The majority of the participants identified feeling a deep pain during their divorce experience, some due to the loss of the relationship; others due to loss coupled with seeing the pain their children experienced. Ideally, parents will be able to co-parent smoothly; however, that is not always the case. From Mary's perspective, her divorce was "amicable," so she was able to share with clients that collaborative co-parenting is possible. She also shares that she is able to understand their fears and anxieties surrounding this.

Mary is able to identify that some of her personal experiences do impact her work and some do not. Although she identifies having her own religious beliefs, Mary feels that her belief "doesn't affect my opinion on divorce or how I counsel families or couples." When Mary meets with a couple who has a story similar to hers, she does have to be self-aware that her own past experience doesn't impact her work:

> If I am being honest, when I see a couple that I can relate to in some way, I just kind of . . . I think I almost have to catch myself to not make assumptions. But, I'm real cognizant of that, like if I see something and almost similar to my situation I think if anything I am more like, I try to find the differences and I don't want to make assumptions. Or I might say, 'Oh this situation is similar to mine,' and it gives me some insight also trying to find the differences so I won't make assumptions. It makes me more aware of being open to what's going on. So, I think for me the similarities are that this was a young couple with kids and she was frustrated, she wants her husband to be home more, but the difference is I could see that see she was trying to control him. That really wasn't my thing so I was kind of listening trying to figure out how I could help them or where I could go with them or make those connections or build those kind of, you know understanding and compassionate relationship with them, and so I think it helps if they know you can connect with them, but, you know, like I said, I try to be cognizant of those differences so I can remove myself from that.

Is My Own "Stuff" Getting in the Way?

Because the pain of the divorce still appears to be very raw for Martin, it would seem that there might be an impact for him if a couple does have a similar story. As he shares his insight, I can hear the disappointment in knowing that he is trying to help clients to identify and resolve their issues while he was unable to achieve the same success for himself:

> Yeah, I mean it is always me checking in with myself and my own emotions, my own experience, as I'm hearing these couples act in ways that my former wife and I acted. The cycle of anger and then just withdraw. And I try to help them see their cycle, their patterns, but again what comes up is like that 'I knew I couldn't do it then.'

Barbara has an interesting perspective regarding the impact of the *similar story* and her relationship struggles. She correlates the impact of the divorce experience to any experience that is similar to any other life event we might experience:

> I don't see that as any different than . . . I have a twin, so I don't see that as any different than if someone says, 'I have a twin and this is how we get along.' I really don't. In other words, "I might pause in session and let my thoughts go to that, but it's almost like meditation. When I meditate I let the thought come in and then I let it go out." But then I am ultra-focusing . . . same thing with divorce as with any issue, it's—to me, it's a process of I pause before I respond and then I consider, would there be anything helpful if the opportunity presents itself to share any of this? And so, my mind automatically goes to 'How could this help this particular person' or 'Would it have any negative impact on our relationship if I did share and am I holding back?' That's the other piece, because I know sometimes if it is a personal issue I would be more likely to hold back. And I'm not just talking about disclosure, I'm talking about everything . . . like emotionally investing in the process with my clients so if I'm holding back am I being 'ungiving' of myself to my client because of a personal issue and if I come to that conclusion,

then I say to myself, 'Grow up, process this a little bit and get rid of it because your client needs you.' It's a self-talk but I really don't look at it any differently than any other issue. And that could be because I've been divorced for 11 years and that I could be far enough removed that the emotional piece is not there. I think I would be more likely to react to something that is 'more fresh' or currently going on in my life.

Corey was not working as a counselor at the time of his divorce, so he has never felt that "his stuff" from the divorce impacted his work. Corey is aware that at times clients have stories that have some similarities to his, but he does not feel those make much of an impact:

I think it probably does but I don't think it changes a whole lot. At times, I think it can but it's not as . . . I think it would have if I hadn't done work through it. I mean, I notice it sometimes, it kind of maybe is familiar, but it's not a . . . I don't know if it's overwhelming, I don't think it affects the work as much as it does maybe remind me I could have done it more differently myself than what I do with them.

The pain and distrust from the relationship with his ex-wife infiltrated Corey's thoughts and feelings about the prospect of successful relationships. He found that he had become despondent in a possible future with any partner and the "notion" of a love story with a happy ending.

I even got bitter about romantic love in a way because it was so many things to it. Almost more like angst than healthy love or attachment that Hollywood kind of perpetuates so I got really frustrated with that. And just kind of got to this place of what in the world. . . . I don't know if you can trust people nowadays. I just went through all these stages of just kind of painful, frustration, anger, and mistrust. Even watching movies or songs, it was kind of this place where like 'Man that's . . .' I guess I was just really sensitive to how bad it could get so then I don't want to do that. So, I ended up really trying to avoid. Even movies, like

I said, I guess stuff like that. But all of it kind of got lumped together in this place of like pain and mistrust.

If Corey had been seeing couples at the time of his divorce, would that "bitterness" somehow have impacted his work with clients? If he was so wounded and despondent that he avoided romantic movies, would meeting with a couple in some way trigger that same need to avoid? Would that lead to him shutting down a couple or perhaps providing more of an educational lecture than a counseling process?

Catherine had been working as a mental health professional for many years by the time of her divorce and she continued to meet with clients during her divorce. She expressed feeling that she had never had a client's story that was "overtly the same" as her own. Some have had "larger themes that were the same." After a pause, she continued:

> It certainly impacts me; I can't say that it doesn't. The couples that are struggling to get it right. By the time some of the couples get to me, they are court ordered to see me because of their ridiculous behavior with one another and any time you see one of those couples . . . I guess that is the one time when I am doing divorce work, when I see some-body with sort of their hands up like 'Make it stop!', that's the one place that I heavily identify with that person and I have to keep myself in check.

Catherine works with many "high conflict" couples. As someone who experienced a "high conflict" divorce, Catherine is aware of the possibility of experiencing more triggers when working in the role as parenting coordinator than couples counselor but does not feel it influences her goal in working with couples:

> Yes, I definitely think that it does [trigger] because I work with highly conflictual couples and I am probably a little bit more biased and I do say it out loud with the couples. That when there are younger children that sometimes the fantasy of divorce, seems like it would be easier if

they were divorced. And I will say out loud that my experience certainly has been that divorce does not make things easier. It's just a new set of problems to deal with, and so I will say that out loud. It's not that I'm against divorce with small children, but I try to be realistic about what they are going to be looking at. And the fact that what I see, interestingly enough in my divorce work, it is not therapy, but it can be therapeutic, is that you see that negative interactional cycle basically on steroids. They become very reactionary with one another and very suspicious, you know, 'Why aren't you more like me?' and 'Why doesn't he or she see it the way that I do?' and very often I will draw out the negative interactional cycle on my white board for them and just say this is probably what was going on in your marriage. We are not going to be doing this in here but let me just show you what happens. And my role a parenting coordinator, in my view, is to be there for the kids and that I'm sort of their advocate.

Valerie is passionate about *being present* in the therapeutic process. That skill requires the therapist to be to be constantly checking in with themselves in order to keep their *own stuff* or beliefs out of the process. Valerie has become proficient at this skill and does not feel that anything in particular comes up for her when a couple's story is similar to her experience:

> I tend to try to, kind of like what you just did and dig into their beliefs. I just, I don't feel like and I've looked at this several times because I think it's so important that I don't impose on them what I would do. You know, but yet on the other hand, I don't start to . . . I don't shy away from that tough stuff they are in either. If that makes sense?

Nick had been in the process of divorce for 10 months, so I would imagine that the emotions are easily triggered surrounding this issue with a high risk for his stuff to enter the room, and I wondered if clients found out he was in the process of divorcing whether he would be able to discuss that without becoming emotional. In spite of all of this emotional turmoil, Nick feels he was able to keep his pain out of his counseling work. His clients did not become aware of his divorce until months after the divorce process had begun. He was able to identify that clients with similar stories do bring up specific emotions and thoughts for him:

It brings up a lot. My immediate reaction is to really appreciate how hard it is. How really, really difficult it is with the dynamics that they are dealing with. On the other hand, having gone through what I've gone through, ironically, I have more hope [laugh]. It's very surprising because I see where our marriage should have gone; I see where it could have worked out eventually.

In reconnoitering his divorce experience, Nick is able to see how his new insight is into times he might notice his own story popping up in a session with couples:

This really gave me clarity and an appreciation and sensitivity to what other people are going through in various crises. Holy crap, something as simple as a client saying, 'I emailed my wife and she didn't respond today'—I would think 'What's the big deal'? Now I can see how—the really big deal—these seemingly inconsequential things have powerful meanings. So, in some ways I am a lot more sensitive and better at some of the cases I was working with, but sometimes I could tell I was going overboard. And, yep, that's it.

In a different case, Nick had concerns that this particular client would have some transference issues if he found out about his divorce:

This week I did disclose to a client who was in the middle of getting a divorce. I very consciously decided that I was going to wait until the end of the session so that this discussion didn't preempt the session. This was a client who had returned to therapy after being away for two years. And he is connected to some friends. He didn't know about it. We didn't have such an intimate relationship meaning that I didn't sense there was an outrageous amount of transference. That was the big concern to me when revealing this to clients: what it does to the transference. What's it do to their image of me? With another client, he was like, 'Well, I feel so sorry for you.' And I said, 'Please don't, this marriage needed to end, it is the right thing, the right choice.'

This issue of transference was important to Nick in his decisions to disclose the divorce information with certain clients. He has also had to navigate times when others have disclosed the information to his clients:

One client found out; two clients figured out inadvertently that I was getting a divorce and confronted me about it. I was immediately honest, there was no question I was going to be honest. 'Yes, I am,' and we had to spend about 10 minutes talking about their concern for my wellbeing. But all of them were extremely compassionate and sensitive. Literally, one of them literally saying, 'I care about you and I'm worried for you.' The client's issue in therapy was always to take care of people. I had to say, 'You don't have to take care of me on this' [laugh]. 'This is where we don't go and that's why I hadn't let you know; it was helpful to have significant time pass. This really occurred 10 months ago so it's not like I'm in the middle of the freshness of it.' And that was really important to me—to get through the initial stage when I didn't want anybody to know.

CHAPTER 6

DO I HAVE WISDOM TO SHARE? AM I CREDIBLE?

During times of struggle and pain, as humans we look to the *experts* for guidance and wisdom, choosing professionals who have been trained in how to repair and save relationships. As mental health professionals, we are trained in theories, skills, and the *process* of counseling; we become *the experts* of the art of communication and repairing relationships. So, our own relationships should be perfect, *right*? Surely, these professionals would have the perfect relationships because they have the knowledge and skills to achieve that elusive bliss and contentment. Certainly, we should be able to navigate and repair any issues that arise with our own marriages and partnerships. When our own relationships falter and unravel, do we lose our credibility to help others? Should we consider ourselves phony and charlatans because we could not get right for ourselves? Or, do we gain wisdom that can help others to avoid the pitfalls we experienced in our failed relationships? If we are also swimming in a muddy pool of personal mistakes and have at times *missed the boat*, many questions arise for clients:

> Do I have confidence this person will know how to help me? Are they confident in their own ability to swim? Because they are swimming with me in the water, can they better understand my fears and panic? Can I trust they will guide me in the right direction?

The majority of colleagues that I spoke with, including the participants of the study, feel that any life experience of the therapist has the ability to benefit our work with clients. We have first-hand knowledge that helps us to empathize and understand our clients. However, all questioned whether clients would feel the same. As human beings we are drawn to relationships and connections with others; we seek companionship and find comfort in the touch of a hand. Experiencing a happy, connected, and successful relationship actually improves our health and life expectancy. So, getting it right is almost vital to our survival.

Before I began my research, I had many conversations with other mental health professionals who were either divorced, getting divorced, or contemplating divorce. Even those in "good relationships" had experienced times of trouble in the relationship, when they just could not unravel and reveal the reason for the discourse. Should those who continue to endure in distant, unhappy, and disconnected relationships be more credible as couples counselors than those who have not remained in a marriage? What exactly ensures credibility and wisdom in a mental health professional who chooses to work with couples? Does it mean that married clients only want to meet with a therapist who has experience with maintaining a successful marriage?

I know my family and friends find humor in the fact that I am a counselor at all, let alone one that focuses on working with couples. And that I actually teach classes and provide workshops for other therapists who are learning to work with couples is astonishing to them. Even more surprising is that I have stood in front of dozens of couples, leading workshops for them on how to connect and improve relationships. Should I consider myself an imposter and possibly go back to the nursing profession where no one cares if I successfully navigate relationships? (I have often considered that.) After talking with many colleagues and their family members, I don't think I am unique in this place of questioning my clinical skills and expertise based on my personal relationship accomplishments (or lack thereof).

Do I Have Wisdom to Share? Am I Credible?

I have actually never had an experience with a client in which my credibility was challenged. I have never worn a wedding ring in session (even when I was married) in an effort to avoid clients trying to guess anything about my personal life. Interestingly enough, I have also never been asked about my marital status. When contacted by clients, 100% of the time I am asked about my training in couples therapy and how much I charge. In sessions, I might get asked if I understand what they are going through, which I do. I actually can understand the desire to hang in there until there is nothing left to *hang on to* and the total disappointment but relief of letting go. I honestly believe I have some wisdom to share.

Along with many of the clinicians that I interviewed, I feel that the divorce experience has the potential to give therapists a unique perspective and wisdom to work with others who are struggling in their relationships: in essence, a *credibility*. I understand this thinking might be perplexing to some, but I believe that our battles and wounds have taught us lessons and provided insight that genuinely might be beneficial to others. As survivors of failed relationships, we are credible witnesses to a tragic crash and burn that we hope to save our clients from experiencing.

Kyle has been remarried throughout his counseling career, so the vast majority of his clients are unaware that he was previously married. Although he feels his divorce experience has provided him with wisdom he can utilize when working with couples and families, he has never experienced a situation when his credibility was questioned.

Catherine has only had one instance where she recalls a client questioned her credibility as a couples therapist:

> I did have one gentleman that after we had been working together for almost three months, I had not self-disclosed, but he heard through the grapevine that I was divorced and came in and said 'What the hell, why should I go to you? If you are divorced why should I come to you, how are you going to do it any better?' Interestingly enough, he did stay and we worked through that and it was fine. My reasons for not

telling him was I felt that the public's perception of me as a divorced therapist would question my credibility. But, I just found it was easier for me just to tell people on the front end and if that presents an issue for them then I am happy to refer to one of my colleagues. I actually have never had anyone take me up on that offer. I think in the beginning I was worried and now I am just much more comfortable with it. I think I just put it out there in the beginning and I have not seen any difference.

Valerie definitely feels her ability to connect with the client in that place of struggle is a wisdom that is due to her own relationship experiences:

It's interesting because I feel like I could relate well to what my couples were going through. And because I did not feel so much as this was the devastation of my life. It was—for me, divorce had some degree of a liberating feel to it. I was in touch with the part of me that wanted to just get out now. And the part of me that couldn't yet. So, I felt that I could kind of hear that in a client. They are in the therapy session with you but they are also—often they come in as a last resort. Not always, but often, one at least has a foot out the door, more often than not. And so, being able to hear that part that wants to leave and the part that wants to stay and not just the part that wants to leave or not just the part that wants to stay. And I felt like I heard, I learned about that in a way through my own experience. I felt like I had heard myself somehow and continued to hear myself. So, wherever that came from on the front end allowed me to relate and hear the struggle and respect the struggle. And be present with them.

Valerie shared a story about a session with one couple in particular. The husband was having difficulty being "present" for the wife. During one session, she got up and left for 10 minutes. When the client returned, Valerie processed her leaving and the client asked, "What happens to you when things like that happen?"

Valerie felt her response was a result of her own divorce experience and struggles:

> I want to be right here with you. And there's just not a part of me that wants to get up and go. Or if there is it's so small that I can handle it. I can sit with this part that wants to stay.

She was able to expand on her feelings as to why she was able to sit with her clients in that scary place:

> So, I just think that the sticking it out as long as I did until I couldn't anymore, until it wasn't an option anymore, helps me to stick out the tough times with the couples and help them to see they can. So, it's kind of like leaning on someone until you can see you can do it yourself. And that's why I like . . . and I don't look for the conflict, I just know that through the conflict is where the good stuff is going to come from. So, I like the conflict because, not that it feels great, because I know, I believe what can come from it. I don't know if that answers your question.

Nick has been a therapist for more than 30 years and before now he had never questioned if clients would doubt his credibility as a counselor. I can see the pain and sadness in his face as he shares this part of his story. I offer to take a break from the interview, but he feels he is "okay." He went on to describe his divorce:

> I think one of the hardest things is that it's very hard for me not to be embarrassed that I'm getting a divorce. It's very hard for me to have to publicly admit a failure, even if it's not 'my fault.' I think it's because it's always my fault at some level; it's always my fault. 'Well I joined in this marriage, I chose that, how can I just blame her?' Or, 'How can anybody just blame him?' You chose this, so you need to take responsibility for how you chose it. So, there is no absolving responsibility in a divorce. There's no 'Oh, I'm the good guy and they are the bad guy.' Or maybe 'I got the white hat and they got the black hat' [laugh]. So

to sit in front of a client and say, 'Yes, I'm divorced.' There's always a feeling of embarrassment for me, a feeling of not good enough, of vulnerability. And it's my job in the session, if it comes up and it's out there, as to how to present it as positive vulnerability rather than negative vulnerability. I'm just human and made some mistakes and I need to own them and 'It was a marriage that needed to end' is sort of the presentation I have.,

Barbara feels that most of her clients just assume that she is single, so her credibility is not an issue. She did have an interesting experience with couple who had fired their previous counselor when they found out she was in the middle of a divorce:

They said, 'Well, yeah, we did see somebody and it was terrible and it didn't work out well and then we found out she was going through a divorce while she was trying to counsel us. What kind of counselor sees somebody for a marriage if they are going through a divorce?' But I thought that was very interesting. What also was interesting was that they didn't ask me if I had ever been married, they didn't ask me if I was divorced. They didn't ask me anything. I do wonder about that.

One particular couple asked Barbara if she had been divorced because one of the spouses had been previously married. In this case, the fact that Barbara was divorced gave her more credibility:

Would it help you to know if I'm married or not or whether I had been? And they both said, 'Yes, it would help us.' And I said, 'How would that help you?' They said, 'Because it shows us you are a human being and shows us you're vulnerable,' something along those lines. And I told them . . . It came up later with them: 'you know the divorce process . . .' But it was not in any kind of . . . it probably built our relationship better. It amounted to . . . I tried handle it in a particular way, and they did as well, they did their part in this as well.

Do I Have Wisdom to Share? Am I Credible?

Corey works a counselor in both a private practice setting as well as a church setting. I wondered if clients in a faith-based community might place expectations on those they seek for marriage counseling and his credibility might be questioned:

> I work with largely a faith community and so I thought at times, I think I feel a little bit more trepidation in sharing because I'm wondering, 'Well, are they going to judge me or say something bad about me or whatever?' I've never had anybody get real frustrated with me about it or tell me, heck, they don't want to meet with me because of it. But I have had people say they appreciate that I'm just real. You know that 'I'm not hiding stuff' and that sort of thing. And so, I haven't had a negative experience with it. All my experiences in telling people about it, like I said, I don't tell them every single detail unless they want to know, and that hasn't really happened that often either. Normally they just say, 'Oh, okay, we are here for our issues, but I'm glad you told us.' And it kind of normalizes their struggle.

Mary does identify feeling that her divorce experience has helped her in her work with families. Her experience has in some ways given her credibility:

> My divorce experience definitely helps me in working with couples because I have had the experience of being married; I've had the experience of trying to co-parent and work with somebody. I've had the experience of effective communication versus no communication whatsoever. And I think sometimes when you can personally understand the frustration that your clients are feeling, it just helps you be a little bit more understanding and able, you know, like you said, when we provide those interventions, help them figure out whatever interventions are needed to help them reach whatever goals they are trying to reach. I'm grateful for my experience and I don't know if I could be as . . . I don't know if I could really understand them if had never been married or never gone through any of those things.

Martin does feel that his clients can in some ways benefit from the wisdom he has gained in his marriage and divorce experiences: "And I think what I could add to that is that I learned a lot from my divorce and that I didn't have these tools that I'm helping you learn. During that time, maybe it could have made a difference." Martin only recalls a few specific clients who were impacted by the news of his divorce:

> I would have to explore that, but the general memory is that there have been some clients who ... especially like more 'staunch' Christian based couples who feel very disappointed by that. And I think there are also some couples where one may, one of the partners may not like having to come to counseling because he or she has been drug there, so it gives them some ammunition to say this is 'BS,' he couldn't even be married. So, there have been times. But for the most part, people don't ask. For the most part—but there is always wonder in me, if they wonder about it and what they think. Sometimes I wonder if they think I'm gay, and, you know. So, I don't address it unless it has to be addressed for some reason.

However, Martin understands why clients might question whether he is a credible couples therapist. He often experiences feelings of "shame, guilt, and embarrassment" that he "couldn't do it better" even though he had been a therapist for 35 years by the time of his second divorce: "It's embarrassing, changed my life in a flash."

Martin did share a particularly moving "credibility" story; a time when he worked on a radio talk show that discusses mental health issues. The event forced him to explore that others might have an issue of credibility around his being a divorced mental health professional:

> I remember being on a radio show that I did for years. Just on mental health issues of any kind and sometimes we would talk about couples' issues. And one time I was talking about what makes a marriage good, what are some of the qualities of a good marriage and then when a marriage dissolves what typically happens and how does it feel. And I was

Do I Have Wisdom to Share? Am I Credible?

right on the brink of sharing that I was divorced and the interviewer, and this is on the radio so visually no one saw, but I was right on the brink of saying that I am divorced and giving some points about that, and she knew it, she could see it in my eyes. I had been doing interviews on the station for years, so the interviewer knew me and she went [motioned to stop]. She motioned with her hands to stop. And so, I got it, and of course I didn't say it, and then what do you do with that? I walked away with, 'Yeah, it's pretty shameful, I guess, my credibility would not be perhaps not be as important or as valid.' Credibility is the thing, whether it's on the radio or individually with my clients.

In spite of the pain and embarrassment from this radio experience, Martin shares that he is somewhat reassured in his credibility as a couples counselor by the fact that many famous clinicians, who in fact have developed theories and models for couples therapy, have themselves been divorced:

You know one thing that helped me just recently is just remembering that Harvel Hendricks was divorced, John Gottman was divorced, Sue Johnson was divorced, and I'm sure there are other couples counselors that were divorced. Many other wonderful writers and people I respect, like the person who wrote *The Power of Now*. I think that helps me to realize that others [therapists] have experienced this. In fact, I was listening to something in the last few days, in preparing for a couples workshop, it was a discussion where even John Gottman was talking about after his divorce and how he began to open up to meet new people.

CHAPTER 7

TO TELL OR NOT TO TELL

Self-disclosure is a complicated variable in the therapeutic process. Since the time of Freud, therapists from all backgrounds have researched this phenomenon, and still there is no real consensus. Depending on your theoretical framework, your belief may be that self-disclosure can have adverse effects or positive influences on the therapist-client relationship.

During times of crisis, therapists are encouraged to explore whether they are able to adhere to their theoretical perspectives or have their boundaries weakened and they begin disclosing too much to clients. If I believe that self-disclosure is an essential element in building the therapeutic alliance, am I attuned as to how, why, and when do I share? If I live in a small community, I am worried that my clients will find out my personal information through the rumor mill? Research does show that it is important to only self-disclose information that will benefit the client in some way (Bass, 2007; Karson, 2008; Karson & Fox, 2010). So, the question becomes, "Am I sharing for me or for the client?" If therapists are meeting with clients to "counsel" and discover new ways to view and resolve issues, should the therapist share thoughts based on their own mistakes in their marriage?

Self-disclosure can be tricky; the label should definitely read "Use with Caution." Some mental health therapists adhere to a policy of

91

non-disclosure; others might struggle with knowing when to stop. I am comfortable with self-disclosure, but I hope I am always mindful to share only for the benefit of the client. As I interview the participants in my research, I do question whether there have been times that I disclosed for the benefit of me.

Interestingly, I realize that my disclosure is never about my marriage struggles or divorce; clients simply don't ask, so I don't tell. Because I do mention insights I have learned from "family" relationships, is there just an assumption that I am married? I am comfortable with disclosure that benefits the client and I find that 99% of my disclosure is snippets of challenges I have experienced with my children or my own parents. In my attempts to normalize human behaviors and relieve anxieties, I share stories of how I make mistakes with a quick and sharp word towards one of my children. I share stories of the difficulties of setting boundaries with family members (and how my adult children set boundaries with me). My clients always respond with relief from knowing that perfection is not a requirement to be considered "normal" and have "healthy relationships."

Some of the participants share that disclosure is a major concern with clients. They worry that if they don't disclose their divorce status, their clients might feel they are hiding a dark secret. Some worry that if they don't disclose the information, their clients will somehow find out later and be angry with them for being "deceived." Martin becomes very serious and intent when sharing his thoughts about disclosing his divorce to clients or colleagues:

> And then, I guess, sometimes, and this is through the years too, and certainly in the last three years inclusion, I don't wear a wedding ring because I'm not married, and so here I am asking couples to share their vulnerability, and I'm talking about the specialness of a relationship and how we heal in marriage and in committed relationships and how worth it is to do it—to go through it and give everything you can to see if that can happen. And, you know, I'm thinking they don't see a wedding ring on me, and I don't say 'my wife,' and I . . . And when I do a

To Tell or Not to Tell

workshop for couples, I think the same thing: 'You got to know I don't have a wedding ring on, I'm sure you're wondering if I'm married.' And I'm certainly not going to be dishonest and act like I'm married, and yet I have a choice. I have to think it through. Like, am I just going to phrase things in ways that could be taken maybe that I'm married or maybe that I'm not, you know, sort of neutral? Or do I just come up front and say, you know, I am divorced so that I want you to know that.

When Martin does disclose his divorce to his clients, he feels he takes into account the reason for the disclosure:

I try to figure out if that would help the couple or not to know. Sometimes they outright ask, and of course I could ping-pong that back and say, 'Why do you ask?' and such as that. Sometimes I disclose, depending: 'What would that mean to you if I were and if I wasn't?' and talk about it that way. But sometimes I just say, 'Yes, I am, yes I am.' The other interesting thing is that sometimes people still will just assume that I'm married even though I don't have a wedding ring on and I don't talk about my wife. But other times, like 'Are you and your wife going on a vacation this summer?' or 'Have you and your wife been there?' I may sometimes say, 'I'm not married; I'm divorced.' That puts me in another difficult position, do I just . . . If it's just a point that I'm illustrating I may not even address that; I may just stay with the concept that we are talking about. Whether my wife and I didn't do it or not, it's just not important, so I just don't address it; I stay with the point. And, then sometimes they say, 'Oh, I'm sorry.' And then, you know, as a therapist, you are left with, 'Oh that's ok,' or having to deal with whatever their feeling might be. So, generally, I hate it [laugh], but I do know that all life experience is valuable and I learned a lot from my first marriage and divorce.

Even three years after his divorce, disclosing his divorce to his clients continues to bring up emotions:

The same questions come up: 'Should I share?' To be honest and open with the clients . . . I'm asking them to be honest and open. Should I

93

share? I want to be authentic. Another thing that I wonder is, 'How many people know that I'm divorced?' and they are just not saying it out loud. It's a small town, so it's another issue of me thinking, 'What do people know about me?' and questioning how honest to be, how open to be, and what's appropriate and what's not, what's helpful and what's not helpful to them. But also: What's fair to myself?

Catherine feels that if clients inquire, she needs to be honest with them regarding her marital status, so she does disclose her divorced status with most of her clients:

I disclose almost, I wouldn't say every couple, necessarily, but I think I'm getting close to every couple. It's just when I do my initial speech about who I am, and my life and work experience. I kind of put that out there. It felt to me that I was keeping a secret and I didn't like that feeling.

Catherine practices in a fairly small community and is cognizant that she and her clients might often cross paths with her in a non-professional setting. Perhaps this lends itself to disclosing more information that clinicians in larger communities might not feel needs to be shared. Of course, in small communities, anonymity is sometimes difficult to maintain. Although Catherine feels her religious beliefs do not influence her work and goals with clients, she will disclose her religious affiliation if clients inquire:

I tell them at the very beginning—for some of the devout Catholic couples, they may have issue with this—but I tell people right at the very beginning that my personal belief is that my role therapeutically is not to save the marriage. My role is for them to understand each other on a different level and to be able to speak with one another at a different level and after that it is up to them. There have been a couple of couples that were devoutly Catholic and initially had a little push-back with that, and I happily would refer them to a Christian Counselor who,

To Tell or Not to Tell

maybe their role and belief system, is much more of keeping the couple together.

Mary will disclose that she is divorced, but it is "situational." In fact, when she chooses to disclose, she is hoping to have an impact. She particularly discloses when there are children involved:

> If I talk with parents of children who are dealing with co-parenting or custody issues, I've disclosed my divorce; when I'm trying to help them try to co-parent or help them try to make decisions in the best interest of the children, I've disclosed it. I think it helps clients to see that there is a way to co-parent. You can work it out, it can happen. That is always that goal [disclosure] and I think it has had an impact.

Nick had managed to hide the divorce from his clients for a while. However, living in a relatively small community where clients know "friends of friends," a mental health professional might not always be in control of the disclosure:

> I only had one client I directly let him know because we have mutual friends. I said to him, 'I don't want you to go home and find out from other friends that I am getting divorced.' I told him I did not want him to hear from anyone but me because I thought that was really important. I said, 'I'm not trying to hide it from you as much as protect you.' And he was appreciative of that and it went well.

Nick recalls one embarrassing moment with a client when the client inadvertently heard about his divorce through his roommate who works in a restaurant:

> My soon to be ex-wife was talking about our divorce in a public place where one of the workers overheard some of the conversations; that worker's roommate was my client. So, this worker goes home and says to my client, 'Well, let me tell you about your therapist.' And so,

95

the client reported back to me all this trash talk. Now it was really fortunate I could look at him and say, 'You know, if those things were accurate, I would be really nervous [laugh].' It was such a pain in the ass at first to have hear, 'Oh, I heard all about you' kind of thing. It was like, jeez, really, now I have to go through this [disappointed sounding].

For the most part, Nick has decided not to let clients know unless "somehow it naturally comes out." If he "anticipates it's going to come up," he might say to his client that, "We might have an issue coming up down the road and it's my job to help you deal with it." Nick feels that he has to be "as honest as possible and forthright and don't hold back." It is his hope that his clients will be able to "handle whatever it is that comes." Nick is mindful that if clients find out he is divorcing, they might see him as leaning towards encouraging them to end their marriage.

With the other client I mentioned, it's been interesting for him. He was divorced before and it was the most dreadful period in his whole life and so he's been really sensitive. He said, 'This must be so hard and so awful.' And right now, he has a horrible marriage, a really tough marriage. And so, I think every once in a while, he consciously or unconsciously tests me by saying 'Maybe I should just divorce her,' thinking that's his solution because that was my solution and he's going to join in my world. And in those cases, I'm adamant, saying, 'No, I don't think you should divorce her, this isn't it, there may come a time down the road where you think this won't work, but not now.' I want to be adamant that he doesn't experience me as secretly trying to join my club of divorcees and think that I think that's the solution to all problems. So, with him I've had to be very vigilant and pay attention to when little sneaky signals come up of 'What do you do about dissatisfaction in a marriage and is divorce the ultimate answer?' I just keep saying in whatever ways I can, 'You want to give this marriage your all, you want to really to give it everything. The grass is not necessarily greener on the

TO TELL OR NOT TO TELL

other side.' And they have such a great life together that their conflicts are painful, but they are not evil.

One of Nick's clients hinted that perhaps Nick saw divorce "as the answer to dissatisfaction" in a marriage and perhaps he should "join Nick's club of divorcees." For the most part, Nick expressed feeling a "sense of embarrassment" at times when either he disclosed or clients become aware he is divorcing:

> But there is still this embarrassment of, ok, I have to wait and see how they receive it, are they going to be judgmental? No matter how clear I am, they may have 'judgmentalness.' It's like, 'Oh, your father is Jewish, I can't see you because I'm a Christian.' So, like 'Oh you're divorced,' therefore, according to them, you don't know how to make relationships work. Ironically, I feel like I'm better at making relationships work because I am getting divorced. Because I played it till the end. But there is a slight embarrassment, and when I'm confronted, there is this immediate feeling of 'Oh shit, I've been caught with my hand in the cookie jar.' You now know something about me that I wasn't necessarily excited to have you know [laugh]. Equally, at the same time, there is also freedom, like 'Oh good, I don't have to worry about this anymore [laugh]; you already know, the cat's out of the bag—yippee!' It's like now I can just move on and if you're still here then you are still here, so I guess you have accepted it on some level, and the more we get to know each other, the more you'll get to know. So, I think it's this back and forth between embarrassment and slight shame and . . .

In spite of some negative experiences, Nick does feel that disclosing his divorce has at times been beneficial to his alliance with clients. One client in particular stands out for him:

> Yes, so one client I let know and he seemed to be fine, I trust he was fine. He's an AA member, and you know AA members are all like, 'You know, we are all knuckle heads here just doing the best we can.' So, I think it

helped that alliance with him in saying, 'You know, I'm not different than you are, we're just co-creating solutions here. I'm not the expert, to a certain extent, but not really, it's more like I'm the co-chair or facilitator,' and so I think it helped us in a way with our alignment.

Although Corey had not been working as a counselor when he divorced, now as a counselor, he does share with clients that he has been divorced. He finds his disclosure has had a "more positive" impact on his work with clients than a "negative impact":

> Most of the time in my initial intake session, I cover my informed consent and all that stuff and then I tell them about myself. And I always say that if there is anything they want to know about me, they can ask about it. Generally, I quickly say, if this comes up or if this is a question, I will say, 'I've been divorced, I've moved a lot, I've had a lot of life experiences, and I'm more than willing to talk about them as much or as little as you want.' But I like people to know up front. I don't want them to find out in a surprising way, so I go ahead and just disclose as soon as I can.

When Valerie began her career, she did not disclose that she was divorced with her clients:

> I didn't at that time much because I wasn't as confident in my role and so there was a couple of times information slipped out from others. Because of the environment I was in, there was a couple of times somehow others learned things about me and I wasn't even the one to disclose it. So, I had to kind of handle that, but I wasn't really big into disclosing my personal experiences other than on a more practical basis. Like how challenging relationships can be but not that I went through divorce, how people can be so different but yet share, but yet love each other and share a common ground. So that's about, somehow, I guess I'm not really remembering it, I remember being more rigid then on what I disclosed until I think I felt like I was—I kind of had it, and then I think some trickled in. Much more [disclosure] now.

To Tell or Not to Tell

In the times that she has disclosed, Valerie can only recall a couple of times when clients reacted negatively to finding out she was divorced:

> I'm thinking there were likely a time or two where someone may have said, or may have alluded to, I'm helping them with their marriage but how much do I actually believe, if I've been divorced. But, I guess because I don't take the position and didn't then, never did, that I'm here to save—you're here to save your marriage, you know. It's, I'm here to support and respect where you are and what you're working through. So, I guess it always seemed to be used for good. Even when it was disclosed by others. I mean, you know, the first experience was "oh, goodness" but then it seemed to shift to something that could be more authentic and provide an opportunity to just be human.

Valerie does feel that the disclosure "ultimately had a positive impact." So, she addressed that she had been divorced with her clients when she felt it was appropriate:

> It wasn't swept under the rug if the information was brought to the table. It was checked in with the client, 'How was that for you to hear that I was divorced?' But, I don't, I'm not remembering any major problems, but there could be something I'm not aware of, right? I mean of couple of my clients might have stopped coming because we're working on a marriage and we are working with a therapist who is divorced. But that's not what my gut is telling me or what I'm remembering. But, again it could have happened without my knowledge.

Since Valerie has been remarried for the past 14 years, she wears a wedding ring so most of her clients don't ask about divorce. However, she does disclose that she is divorced when it is beneficial to the client:

> I certainly can't say I don't at all because it's just too helpful. But it's kind of minimal, necessary information that can be helpful. It doesn't really bring me into their process. And I don't know if I do it with all

99

couples. They're not really talking about divorce a lot of time. They might be talking about the fear of leaving each other, but not always talking about divorce. They might touch on it and turn to where we are now. So, I think maybe the nature of the work I do brings them back into what they are experiencing now. So, I don't know, I think I probably share that I've actually been divorced a little less, thinking about it. Because it doesn't seem as valuable, but I certainly wouldn't say I never do. I just don't—not that rigid.

Since Barbara did continue to work through the divorce process, I wondered if she decided to disclose to her clients what she was experiencing. Her feeling is, "I don't disclose, I am careful with disclosure." However, she reports that only a few clients have inquired as to her marital state:

'Are you married? Have you ever been married? Are you divorced?' So, you get questions and I usually try to field those questions along the lines of 'Yes, I was married.' Just simple, and I might say, 'Are you wanting someone who has gone through the divorce process?' or 'How are you conceptualizing this?' So, I usually do try to turn it back around. I don't necessarily feel defensive talking about it. It's all part of me, it's all who I am. So, if there is information about me that I think could help them ... if they are curious about it. But I am careful though, I am not going to say, 'Oh, I went through a divorce too, I know what it's like.' Absolutely not. I don't think—most of my clients don't ask me. They are ok with not knowing. I think they are ok with the focus being really on what they want and need. I don't think a lot of people know I'm divorced, but maybe they assume that I am and it's not an issue for them. As in they are ok with it either way and it doesn't matter.

Barbara reports feeling that she has never experienced a negative impact on her alliance with a client if they found out she was divorced. She does have a private practice at a home office, and it is her feeling that clients might notice a lack of other cars or other indications or they might access through the Internet that she is single.

Since Kyle was already remarried when he began working with couples, the issue of whether or not to disclose his divorce to his clients did not seem essential in his work with them. Kyle felt very strongly that disclosure must be "in the best interest of the client and not mine." In fact, he could only recall two instances where he did disclose that he could relate to the pain of divorce:

> One in which my therapeutic alliance was being jeopardized tremendously by a wife, a spouse who was very upset because she felt that I didn't understand her situation and was really hurt by her husband's decision to break it off and she felt like I should have been more of an advocate. I remember feeling it was an ok thing to do. I didn't go into detail, I just said—she was essentially saying to me, 'You don't get it, you don't get it'—and I just said, 'I do get it. I've been where you've been and that's all I can say.'

Kyle believed that if he had not disclosed his ability to understand this client's pain, it would have broken the therapeutic alliance: "I can assure you that if I had not self-disclosed in a careful way the information to that client, I would have never seen them again."

CHAPTER 8

AM I MORE LIKELY TO ENCOURAGE DISCONNECTION?

In addition to the training and expertise of the therapist, expectations may also exist about the personal experiences and the beliefs of the therapist and the influence that will have in their work (Tambling et al., 2014). Do some clients seek out therapists who are looking to help them save the marriage at all costs? For some mental health professionals working with couples, there can be a feeling of needing to save a relationship in order have a successful therapeutic outcome. Once you have experienced your own divorce, does the experience itself open the door to a new definition of successful outcome?

For many of us, our marriages preceded our training as therapists. We spent our youth floundering around in unchartered waters like the rest of the "unskilled" inhabitants of the planet; we fumbled through relationships using the skills we learned as children. Often, unknowingly, we "parroted" one of our parents' relationships style, repeating the same mistakes over and over. Now, looking back through a lens that provides clarity to past behaviors and emotions, I have some insight as to why I struggled. But the enlightenment came too late to save my marriage, and it failed (I failed).

Now, as a therapist, am I subconsciously taking on the role of "Captain Fix It" or "Marriage Miracle Worker" for other couples to prove I can help someone get it right? If I work with a couple and the relationship ends, does that bring back those feelings of failure? Do I fight to keep even the toxic and painful relationships together so that it doesn't feel like my own failure?

My colleagues consider me a fairly "pushy" counselor; I hold the flame under the feet of my each of clients in an effort to help them gain agency over their lives. I share that I expect both to identify their own role in the destructive cycles in the relationship and do not identify one partner as "the problem" that needs to "be fixed." I consider myself to be committed to working relentlessly to help clients achieve their goals and I will work as hard as they are willing to work. And I am always upfront with my goals for working with them. I want each individual client to:

1. Gain "insight into why they think, feel, and behave" the way they have.
2. Gain an understanding of what they are doing that is "blocking a connection" in their relationships.
3. Gain "empathy and compassion" for themselves and the other human being in their relationship.
4. Identify their needs and expectations in relationships and be able to share those with their partner.
5. Understand that compromise is essential in navigating a successful relationship.
6. Feel safe in their relationship so they are able to be vulnerable with their partner; to be honest with their deep emptions and allow their partner to "be at the bottom of the well with them."
7. Learn how to accept and repair.

However, I see the couples that other therapists have "given up on," and I am always clear that I will not give up if they are still willing to work, but I do not have a desire to encourage two human beings to continue to inflict pain on each other if we are not able to stop the destruction. And, knowing the impact of parental conflict, I do discuss with couples how their escalations or silences are impacting their children. I am honest that I do not view divorce as a failure.

Kyle was left to be a single parent to his children after his divorce. He identified feeling that this ultimately gave him an opportunity to have a "special relationship" with his children that he would not have experienced if not for his wife leaving. However, he was aware of the pain his children went through in the divorce and he currently remains committed to helping the couple repair if possible: "And that every couple I see that has kids I am very aware of the pain that my kids went through, and that's a reality, so that's always in the back of my mind."

For Kyle, his feeling was that having found happiness in his second marriage likely helps him to feel less pressured to keep a marriage together if the couple is not able to salvage the relationship. Kyle remained single for two years before marrying his current wife of 24 years. It was after marrying again and having a successful relationship that Kyle decided to pursue his career in counseling. He feels that his new relationship has impacted his work with couples in that his second marriage somehow gave him hope:

> There is less pressure when you work with someone like, if you hadn't experienced that pain, and you didn't know that even if they didn't make it, you'd know that there would still be a quality of life that might even actually be a good thing in the long term. If you didn't know that then your sort of . . . oh I have to make this relationship stay together somehow because you might be wondering I pretty much found my happy on the backside of it. So even if they weren't going to make it, I was okay. I mean, I was all in trying to help them but if they didn't I really knew in the back of my mind that they would both be okay because I had come out of it.

Mary identifies her theory base to working with clients as Solution Focused. With that in mind, she approaches counseling by focusing more on the present, what the goals are, and not just on saving the relationship:

> I think the past and what you have been through is important, but I don't dwell there; like my approach is more about what is the presenting issues and, okay, how can we move forward? What do you need from each other in order to help your kids or whatever the goal is. If the goal is to work on the relationship or if the goal is that we have already decided to get a divorce, and we are dealing with how are going to co-parent because I don't like what she has going on over here or I don't like what she is doing. If the goal is to help them try to co-parent, how do we deal with those issues?

Mary was clear that her goal is to meet the clients where they are and to allow them to set the goal for the counseling process. In Mary's divorce experience, she did have younger children at the time of her divorce and does identify that she might offer couples different "interventions" based on the wisdom she has from her own experience:

> I think it depends on the situation and if they are dealing with the fact that . . . you know if it's a money issue and if the kids are the in the house, the dynamics of the situation, if the kids are grown and in the house, that could be a strain on the marriage. So yes, the interventions would be different. If you are dealing with grown kids, who are in the house who are causing the strife on the marriage, maybe I would work with that couple on maybe coming to some agreements on how to help their marriage if that is causing a strain. Versus if it's babies or younger kids in the house issues on money because one partner may be spending or they are not operating within the same budget, so it's different factors that might cause different interventions.

She did further embellish on the possible impact children have on her approach with the couple:

I think maybe my interactions or questions, maybe the process might change if they have younger or older kids. Yes, yes it changes, it depends on the issue and what they are dealing with. Sometimes I can say something to a family that has been married and may have older kids verses new couples who don't have any kids. But as far as my approach, I'm the same with my approach but the situation may change.

Catherine expressed feeling that her divorce experience, her current healthy relationship, and new theoretical framework have all impacted her approach to counseling:

I think being divorced also has . . . you know, I can look at couples. My goal is not to keep them married, but I can look at couples and say being divorced isn't easier. There is this fantasy of 'the pain will stop if we are divorced,' and, particularly when you have children, it sort of is an ongoing thing. But I think understanding both sides of sort what is the terminal detachment in divorce and being in a relationship that is very secure, it helps knowing both sides of that.

Although Corey did not have any children at the time of his divorce, he now is a very proud father. I wondered if this new experience impacts his interventions or focus with his couples. Corey feels that his goals and interventions are the same with couples whether they have small children or not:

I'm always working as hard as I can to save the relationship whether they do or don't have children. Maybe I have some awareness of the pain that the kids will go through because of the divorce, but I don't think I operate differently or approach it differently. You know the divorce affects the kids. You know there is a definite cost there. The kids are the unwitting victims of divorce because they don't have a choice in it and it is basically dissolving their family. I mean, you are separating, so it's different, you know what I mean? You have two different entities that don't exist in the one sense that they used to, so it's altered on both sides. Not only is the mom affected by the pain and grief of the divorce or the dad affected by the pain and grief of the divorce, but now they have to go and figure out how to function individually or separately and make life work. So that changes all the dynamics and then the kids get trapped in two separate rules generally. But most parents that get divorced don't operate very well, on making decisions and resolving conflict already or else they probably would not be getting divorced.

Nick had a teenage child living at home at the time his divorce proceeding began. He does share the insight and wisdom of the impact of divorce on children. In the past, his advice came from research and statistics; now it comes from a more intimate place of pain and experience:

What I heard research-wise is that the percentage of children from divorced families versus the percentage of children from intact families that go into therapy is almost the same. So, divorce in and of itself is not the evil. It's how you relate in the course of that divorce. How you relate to the children, et cetera . . . And there is that adage that when you are flying on an airplane and you have young children that you put the oxygen on yourself first, you can help them get back control, they can't help you get back in control. So, you have to figure out where the balance is between you and them. With older children, I think of it as being less severe, less significant, but still again you want to be able to . . . really what you want to be able to do is 30 years from now you want to look back and say, 'I really gave it everything, I really did the best I could and I tried everything I know how to do.' And so, you have regret but not guilt, not shame, not remorse, but you have regret, like I'm really sad it didn't work, and how do you avoid the guilt, shame, and the remorse—that's the adage.

Nick does feel his view might be different when couples have younger children and for couples with no children:

Yes, so with young children, the statement I use is, 'Look, right now we are talking about your divorce, and you have young children, so my number one concern is your young children.' I will discuss with them that they have the children, and the children didn't ask to be brought into the world, and they are their responsibility. So, on one hand, I will say to them, 'My opinion is that at the end of the day you should be able to look at your children with total sincerity, heartfelt sincerity, and say I did everything I could to make this marriage work. I tried everything I know how to do and really wanted it to work and it just doesn't work.' And then with couples that have no children, I think there is a freedom there to try, in some ways even harder—in some ways you got nothing to lose in either direction, really, except in finances and an empty life. There's a kind of freedom to explore, 'What is it about you that I don't understand?' and 'What is it about me that you don't understand?'

Nick feels that he is very clear with his couples as to what his goals are when working with them:

Whenever I see couples, if it's a couple, my first statement to them is that, 'It's my job to help you guys see the best in each other because right now all you see is the worst in each other.' And your demons are being brought out. And do we shift from a power play to a negotiation and to a collaboration? How do we help you understand each other in a much better light and what's the back stories that are going on here? You see the front stories, you see the symbolism, but you don't see the back stories. But it's more of a sort of evolutionary process.

At the time of his first divorce, Martin did have two young children. He does feel this provides him with wisdom with clients and the future of their relationships. He identifies that his approach is to have empathy for both the parents and the children and what is best for everyone:

Well, I really try to empathize with couples who have younger children because I know the pressures, the exhaustion, of taking care of them. The responsibilities of being pulled in so many directions for childcare, children's activities, sports, dance, whatever it is. And just the exhaustion of baths, dressing, meals, and how it is for them to still stay with their passion and love for each other. The importance of their own couple's relationship. I guess I really try to emphasize and encourage them a lot.

For couples whose children have grown, Martin feels he might try to point out some positives to having the opportunity to work on their relationship at this time in their life.

I emphasize a lot about . . . they have a new lease here. They can create something, anything they want now because they are not bound by having to care for young children anymore, so it's an opportunity to grow and make it different if they choose.

Barbara's daughter was only two years old at the time of her first divorce and in high school at the time of her second divorce. She has twice experienced the immediate impact divorce has had on her daughter as well as the long-term consequences. She identified feeling that younger children in client families impact her work and the direction she offers those couples:

Definitely. Absolutely. It depends on the issues the couples are bringing. I think my interventions are the same for all couples, but I explore what it means to them. What is their belief system? I specialize in working with divorced families, so with that specialized training, I know from the research that divorce is not the end of the world; the children will be fine. But if you two [the parents] are ripping and roaring, these kids will not be fine. So, I share research that says this is up to you two.

Through her experience of divorce and having a young child at the time, Valerie has a clear philosophy and wisdom around children, staying married, and deciding to divorce:

So, what I learned and tend to believe is that divorce is not what devastates children as much as how the divorce is handled and how two people can work through it and, of course, more often than not they're at extreme odds with each other because they feel very betrayed and hurt. But the betrayal and the hurt and the ... what it does, what it can do to the individuals to feel betrayed in that way and how that is passed on to the children is what I'm most concerned about. So, I do keep—so, maybe there is a difference in the way I see it because if they have young children there's—the sensitivity is greater. The sensitivity that we have to take those young children into account, whereas if they don't—so, I'm sure there is a little bit of a difference now that I'm thinking about it. You know, when I have them in the room. I know I went through mediation trainings so sometimes I use that in my work, and I might write their names, the children's names, down on a piece of paper and put it in between them when they are a little bit more escalated because I actually feel like when ...

It's evident this issue is significant to her as she takes a long pause here to really think about her answer:

You know, it's similar to working with someone who may have suicidal ideation, you know ... to hear them but also to see that they are connected to these other human beings [children] that make a difference. That are meaningful to them, they know that they are meaningful to them, but they can lose sight of them. When we have ... in our sight young people that we may be affecting, I think we pay attention a little more. So, yeah, I would say it does make a difference.

CHAPTER 9

MOVING FORWARD

There are those of us whose marriages have sunk to the bottom of the ocean, and there are many who are hanging onto their life preservers just struggling to stay afloat. The experience of being a "couples counselor" living in a marriage or relationship where you are so distant that you can barely remember the touch of your partner seems to be at times more torturous than that of the therapists who have been divorced. Every day these therapists are working with couples to find their way back to that intimate place; helping couples with awareness, connection, communication, conflict resolution, and forgiveness. At the same time, wondering, "If my words can somehow benefit others, why couldn't I find the words to restore that bond in my own relationship?"

As I spoke with colleagues about my research, I was approached by other mental health professionals who shared feelings of what it's like to sit with clients who are in the same boat. Although this was not part of the research for my dissertation, I do feel that in moving forward, the feelings shared by these professionals highlights the continual need for *self-of-the-therapist* work.

Susan has been married to Phil for over 40 years; they have raised their children and have two beautiful grandchildren. Over the years, they have experienced a range of temperatures in their relationship, ranging from warm and comfortable to cold and lonely. Through all the years and changes, Susan has worked diligently with her clients and is a very well respected and popular couples therapist. As with many other therapists that I spoke with, Susan's own relationship struggles become more apparent during trainings and workshops when she is really encouraged to share and examine her own relationship issues. This is the time when our own *disconnections* are illuminated, when we are focused and listening to the *relationship gurus*; our eyes are opened when our minds are quiet and not trying to attune to the client or de-escalate the turmoil in the room. And that's when the pain is noticed.

Charles has been married for the past 20 years and has been working with couples for the past 17 years. Because he feels secure in his marriage, he is always confident in the ability for his relationship to be repaired; he does not experience the same pain as others whose relationships are teetering on the edge. As with most therapists I spoke with, the universe seems to bring him clients with the exact issues he is currently grappling with in his own relationships. He shared that he finds the humor in the irony of this experience and actually leans into the experience. He might even disclose that he understands the struggle they are currently experiencing because he is human and can relate to the same struggle. So, instead of being distracted by his own "stuff," he brings his humanity into the room and uses it in the process with his clients. This is not to say that Charles shares the details of his own family strife; he simply shares that there can be storms in his own relationships, so he understands the couples' plight.

As I move forward in my work as a therapist, I'm *okay* with being a divorced therapist who works with couples in exploring their relationship. I've learned to smile when family and friends make sardonic comments they find humorous. I appreciate the irony of identifying myself as a "couples therapist," when I also have to identify myself as a "divorced woman." In my first career, I was a R.N., so no one really cared if I was married, but now I've chosen a career that reminds me on a daily basis that I "got it wrong."

In the same way that the divorce experience can change beliefs about relationships, the same is true when a new and successful relationship is established after the divorce. Kyle, Catherine, Corey, Barbara, and Valerie currently have healthy and connected relationships. Their new *happy* relationships encourage them to work harder on the self-awareness, accepting what they bring into the relationship and how they can avoid making the mistakes made in their previous relationships. They agreed that the new relationships definitely influence their current work with couples.

All of the clinicians expressed feeling that the more training they received in working with couples, the more equipped they were to be a better partner in their own relationships. And the more hope they were able to share with clients. Corey's training in counseling after his divorce changed some of those hopeless feelings towards relationships and helped him with awareness in his role:

> In going through the training that I've been through, it makes me see my part in it and kind of understand a little more of my non-responsiveness or even a critical "pursuer" at times. I think I kind of did both at different times. I can see my part and see the need, the longing that she had and I had too, and how I could have met that.

Corey met his new wife while working on a Master's degree as a mental health professional. He was connecting with a new relationship and at the same time he was gaining knowledge through his educational experiences in counseling theories. This combination led to his feelings about relationships changing. Corey feels that his current successful marriage influences his work with couples:

> I think it has impacted me some. Just in that I think there is hope. I think if I had not had success in it, I think I might not be working with couples. So, I believe I know what is good and that it can be done whereas in the past I might not have even seen that, so I think I might not have been working with couples if I hadn't had this newer

opportunity. I might have at some level been working with them but not as much as I do. So, I think it gives me hope for them.

Catherine identifies two factors that have recently impacted her current work with clients, "training in an attachment-based therapeutic model and a new successful relationship." She shared that with her recent education in an attachment-based model, she has changed her therapeutic approach with clients from the "old school, long term, restructuring type of therapy" to an attachment-based approach. This provided her with some insight into her failed marriage:

> What I realized is that, when I married into this family structure that is very, very different than mine . . . I am not from here and I am the oldest child, I was the good kid, I was the responsible one, I was very prized in my family, I was the golden child. And I married into this family where the family structure was just very, very different. But learning the new attachment-based theory after I was divorced, I don't regret divorcing; I'm glad I'm divorced from the person I'm divorced from. But I also see my role in that marriage in a much different way. I am much more the Withdrawer and I can see that I just I kept him frenzied because I just kind of kept myself away from him. It didn't feel safe, it didn't feel safe on my honeymoon. Not physically unsafe, emotionally unsafe.

As Catherine discusses her new relationship, the joy beams across her face. She has been in a committed relationship for the past year. She feels that this new relationship has made an impact on her current work with couples:

> Absolutely. I think the biggest thing is the feeling of secure and safe and unconditionally supported and loved. I am in a very happy relationship. Because of the attachment training, I think I am a much better participant in a relationship. Never felt with my ex-husband from the very beginning, and so I knew it wasn't a unicorn. I mean I believed it could happen but it was more a theoretical or intellectual exercise

MOVING FORWARD

and now feeling the feeling of what it actually feels like to have my feet grounded is very different.

Mary's final thoughts are that she feels she has done enough self-exploration of her marriage and divorce to be aware of any residual impact on her work with clients. She does not feel that her own experiences have a negative impact in the session; in fact, she identifies feeling that her divorce experience has helped her with understanding and empathy in her work with families and couples:

> My divorce experience definitely helps me in working with couples because I have had the experience of being married, I've had the experience of trying to co-parent and work with somebody. I've had the experience of effective communication versus no communication what so ever. And I think sometimes when you can personally understand the frustration that your clients are feeling, it just helps you be a little bit more understanding and able, you know—like you said, when we provide those interventions help them figure out whatever interventions are needed to help them reach whatever goals they are trying to reach. I'm grateful for my experience and I don't know if I would be as . . . I don't know if I could really understand them if had never been married or never gone through any of those things.

Nick expanded on this in terms of the divorce bringing a more human element to his role of mental health therapist:

> My sense is that it has so far made me human with the clients. One or two have said, 'Well it just goes to show you that you think your counselor can handle anything and there you are, they got a real life too. They have problems that they have to manage and it doesn't always go well, you can't just solve any problem.' And that's kind of an important realization for people is that you are not a failure necessarily if you can't succeed in a marriage. Some marriages aren't supposed to happen or outlive what they are supposed to be.

Through his own counseling work, Nick has gained some insight into his relationship. He is by nature a storyteller, so he goes on to compare his marriage struggles to an old joke about the irony of expectations we have regarding change:

> You know the joke about the turtle and scorpion. The scorpion is sitting on the side of the river and asks the turtle for a ride and then stings the turtle, and the scorpion says, 'What did you expect? It's my nature.' I just refused to see her nature. Not that her nature is bad, it's just—holy smokes, it's just a different universe from where I am. No wonder we couldn't get along. That makes me want to cry.

Insights gained through his personal counseling experience have helped him get over some of the anger and "get to a place of resolve." This resolve also helps him in his work with couples by clearing up some of the confusion he experienced in his divorce experience:

> So, it looks confusing, but it's helpful to see how confusing it is. Kind of like what you were saying about go deeper into the pain of it just to explore it and see how confusing it is and how unavailable the solution was. On one hand, it's a relief, but on the other hand, it's made me more hopeful to say well until it's really clear in that way you don't want to leave, because if you leave before it's clear in that way you are going to feel guilty or a shmuck or bad and like you didn't give it your all. So, I think one of the only things I guess that's becoming clear to me now while we are talking is the one thing I take solace in is I gave it everything I could: financially, time wise, and heartfelt wise. And that part I feel good about. I feel bad about my stupid mistakes that will bring me shame for the rest of my life. And so, to be able to look at a couple who are struggling or an individual comes in with their spouse. It's kind of like, you actually will get stronger by giving it your all and knowing you've done that so that later you don't second guess yourself and then you go forward with an intensity that has some optimism to it.

MOVING FORWARD

Valerie does believe that her current marriage has impacted her work with her clients:

> Well you know, I always believed that I could be in a successful relationship. I say always—for the most the part I believed I could be in one. So, I really think, I can't imagine it hasn't made a difference. But actually, working with couples influences me to work harder in my marriage and working harder in my marriage influences me to be able to see the struggles and the challenges of couples. So, I think they kind of feed each other. I think for me, doing any other work, I might not be working as hard on my marriage.

Valerie has become an ardent practitioner of mindfulness. She teaches classes, lectures and assists in workshops to help other mental health professionals with self-awareness and self-care. She is committed to "being present" with her clients when they are in their places of pain and struggle. And, she is aware that her past relationship experiences are a vital part of what allows her to be there. She identifies that the "therapeutic presence" is the framework she utilizes in working with her clients:

> I can't imagine being effective at all if I'm not incredibly dedicated and give space to myself to do my own work. Whatever that is for me. But it is therapeutic presence, without that. I mean this is a pretty strong statement but I believe 100 percent. If I cannot cultivate therapeutic presence, I have no chance in helping anyone because it meets them at a level that is necessary for healing, and without that, I'm just helping couples cope. And that might be okay for them, depending on where they are when they come in, they might just need to cope for a while. But if they believe that coping is their answer, they won't ever get to the healing. They are going to struggle and their marriages are going to suffer. So, it's that therapeutic presence that's fundamental.

During the initial interview and in a follow-up conversation, Valerie was very mindful and introspective in sharing her current feelings surrounding her divorce:

> The experience as a whole gave more than it took. Now I can say that the experience as whole gave more than it took. And it allowed for a tremendous amount of empathy. I have a tremendous amount of empathy for me then. And, kind of like an appreciation, a value for me then because it was tough but when you go through go through tough times, they can be liberating. I see and reflect back on it as a time of suffering, initially believing I can't be okay if it's not 'fixed' . . . to feeling the hurt and betrayal, to healing and growing, leaving me with an inspiring life experience that allows me to reach out for her (me then) with appreciation, gratitude, and strength. I don't feel anywhere near the same degree of pain and suffering, minimal to none. I knew then on some level the hurt was healing but it was also very difficult as a single parent and I had to be in it as long as necessary, learning to love myself (aka self-compassion) more and more. This brought me to the healing that ultimately liberated me and gave me a life of great compassion for others, which is a significant part of my effectiveness as a therapist [that] I don't believe I could have had without it. Peace through pain.

Valerie's final thoughts move to the process of healing that can occur in the counseling process:

> We cope a lot in life, we cope a lot in our relationships and it interferes in healing. The healing part is available to all of us if we open our hearts, to the extent that we open our hearts with our pain, our suffering, our vulnerability. So, when we allow someone in that place . . . And I really do believe that in the beginning, and that's why I love the work I do. We [humans] need support, because we don't know how to do it. But when we allow someone into that place, when we allow ourselves to be into it, and allow someone else to witness it, it can soften us. If another can meet us there, it can fully open our hearts in a

way to provide the sense of security, the secure attachment that we can never have otherwise. So, with true intimacy, it requires risk, it requires vulnerability. But we're all innately capable of that. But if you get too stuck in coping, you're still going to suffer and you're not really going to go to each other in tough times . . . You are just going to put, maybe like a Band-Aid. But again, I do think coping skills are important but we still need to get to the place where we can heal. The place where we can at least take the edge off of things so we don't harm each other. But without getting to that much, much deeper place of healing, we are going to still suffer and we are still going to be looking for it somewhere. We're going to still yearn and long for knowing someone has our back because we don't know unless we can show them what we really need. And we are afraid to do that. We are afraid to show our vulnerability.

Martin continues to work on recovering from his divorce experience and moving forward with his life. He continues with his own personal counseling, and is focused on counseling that is more attachment and systems based. Since his divorce three years ago, Martin does date; however, he feels that he in some ways avoids potential committed relationships:

I occasionally go out with the same woman, but I don't feel a draw that it's someone that I'm going to be with forever, or a love relationship that I'm going to develop. And I've been honest about that with her. So, every couple, two to three weeks we will do something and that's it. I haven't really reached out to establish a primary relationship with anybody yet. And I've tended to shy away from others who wanted that from me.

Martin identifies his theoretical framework in working with clients as "attachment based." He feels the interventions in the model he utilizes addresses the "attachment wounds and how the couple plays those out in the relationship." It is his experiences of learning an attachment model and sharing it with others that have provided him with some awareness in a philosophy of working with clients:

> And yet I guess the biggest thing for me is to know, to truly know and I do know all that has happened to me, including both divorces and other losses or experiences in my life, have made me—part of who I am and part of how I can be helpful to other people. So, I think I'll come to more and more peace about that; although I know it will continue to be somewhat of an issue, over time I think it will be less of an issue as I am more peaceful. But it will always be there. I remember Harvel Hendricks said at a workshop when someone asked him if he had ever been divorced, I could see what I interpreted as shame on his face. But what he said is, 'Yes, but if I had known the skills that I'm teaching now, I would not have been.' But he was remarried at that point [laugh].

As time passes in the wake of a failed marriage, so does the reactivity to wounds from the relationship. Barbara has been divorced for almost 12 years, and felt is she now "less responsive" to the possibility of being triggered in a session than when the divorce was still "raw." For Barbara, changes have occurred for both her and her family. Barbara shared that her mother has become more accepting of marriages ending in divorce and is supportive of her current relationship. Barbara no longer practices the Catholic religion. She is now invested in learning about spiritually and growth. When meeting with clients, her own religious beliefs are not brought into the counseling process:

> I study more about other religions that probably resonate more with me now. I don't know, I think it has to come from them not me. I don't think . . . it's almost like sometimes I get this visualization when I work with people. Especially when I know I'm so different from them. It's like I just kind of picture myself as a vessel and what is your belief system is okay so let me feed this back to you.

During the interview, I observed that Barbara sounded a bit sad when discussing her divorce. "Yes, it is even now when I think about

MOVING FORWARD

it; here I sit, I'm actually a little sad." I asked if there was any anger still around her divorce:

> I can only do my piece in this, and you have to do your piece as well, and that's the part that did make me angry for a long time. Now it is just probably sadness, 'Why couldn't you get your act together and just do your part?' 'This is not an unrealistic expectation, this is something we agreed to.' 'How can you say one thing and then do something different and I am supposed to be okay with that?' I mean I wasn't kidding when I said [laugh] this was not something that I could do. . . .

However, she added that: "Because a lot of the marriage it was really me holding down the fort [laugh], he wasn't. So that wasn't fulfilling for me, so I don't grieve that."

As mentioned earlier, Barbara is currently engaged and will be remarrying in a few months. She did feel that her current relationship did in some way impact her work with clients:

> So, does this current relationship enhance my ability to help people bond or resolve their issues? Do I respond any differently? I don't know, I feel like I've been a counselor forever, I feel like I've just done this forever and I feel like it's just . . . maybe I don't reflect on it enough. Maybe I don't put enough thought into it. My life is so fluid I just don't know if it does affect it any more than anything else. I mean when my daughter was pregnant or when my grandkids were born, or when my daughter got married, when I started my own practice. I mean I just don't know if there is anything different in this than in any other of those.

Barbara identifies herself as someone who believes in attachment and system theories. She was intrigued with an ACA book that focuses on the counseling relationship:

> I am always looking for more about family therapy and not necessarily divorce, but possibly. How do our own families, how do our own world

views about our families, how does that impact our clients, how do we see all this? Part of what they said [in the article] was more attachment theory. How we as counselors have to ... Talking about the termination process and how we constantly have to say goodbye to our clients and a lot of time we don't go through a formal termination process because they will come one day and don't come back, and we have to be ok with that. We have to learn how to let go, we have to learn how to process that. We have to let them own that, but at the same time we are human beings too. I think that's a piece of it for couples, that everything they say and everything that we work on impacts me in some way.

Her final thoughts returned to her relationship with her clients and not her divorce:

I don't think I focus on the divorce, to me I don't focus on the ... like in the ACA book on the evidence based stuff in that counselors focus on the documentation and insurance and might forget about the relationship piece. All the fancy interventions are a bunch of 'Hoo-ha.' It's about the relationships and that is what I really focus on and that has always been the most important to me.

Kyle's final thoughts go back to his belief that he would have been a horrible therapist before this happened. "Probably err on the side of justice. Like what's right, who's right and who's wrong. So fortunately, what I got out of that pain was that kind of thinking went away." Kyle feels is now more "open and understandable" to divorce. His new feeling is that "there are just things that happen and sometimes we don't know why they happen, it's hard to accept, to really say we don't know why something happened. It's pretty vulnerable really because if you think you know what happened you can sort of come up with some kind of strategy to deal with it, so yeah."

In exploring this topic with colleagues, the phenomenon of divorced mental health professionals working with couples is more common than I had realized. As a clinician who joined the mental health profession later in life, I was probably among those who thought that the *experts* in communication and expressing feelings would somehow be exempt from the ranks of the fallen. Now, as a clinician whose focus is on working with couples and families, as well as training other clinicians to work with couples and families, it is clear that more research into this topic would be beneficial to the profession.

If future research suggests that clinicians might underestimate the impact of divorce and other life crises on their work with clients, should this become a fundamental and required academic focus in educational programs for mental health professionals? The importance of *person-of-the-therapist* work is merely touched on in most academic programs and not necessarily addressed with the amount of vigor it might deserve. Perhaps mental health training programs should dedicate an entire semester to the students focusing on their own challenges and offer classes in *self-of-the-therapist* and mindfulness. Furthermore, conducting pre- and post-tests from classes or workshops focusing on *person-of-the-therapist* could potentially aid in assessing awareness and knowledge gained by the clinicians participating in the training and direct future research on not only divorce, but many other life experiences.

I believe it is important to note that none of the participants felt they were more likely to suggest divorce as an *easy option* because they were divorced. In fact, even participants who experienced a painful marriage felt strongly that being certain to *give it your all* and have no regrets was paramount to any feelings of contentment with the divorce. It was not surprising to me that participants who have been able to engage in healthy relationships post-divorce have a different and more hopeful outlook than those who have not. Although the new experience provides those participants with hope for happiness in a future relationship, the data does not indicate that they encouraged their clients to consider divorce any more than those participants who were not in a new relationship.

We are all human and emotional beings; we absorb and integrate each and every moment of connection and disconnection as we move through our journey. Despite our valiant efforts, we cannot avoid the reality that we are a culmination of all our experiences. Through the interviews and dialogue with the mental health professionals in this research, the data revealed that these *experts* have an awareness of their humanity, vulnerability, and fallibility. Their experience with divorce does infiltrate every aspect of their life; it has undoubtedly changed perspectives in numerous arenas of their lives. As mental health professionals residing in the bodies of vulnerable human beings, they are committed to utilizing that experience and sitting alongside clients as they navigate the rough waters of life.

The journey of this research has illuminated many aspects of my experience that resonated with feelings of failure and disappointment in those who joined me on this journey. There were times when I saw the tears well up in their eyes and heard the pain in their voices as they shared their stories of loss. Some of the participants had healed and moved forward to a place of happiness and contentment, the new experiences allowing them to share this hopeful place with clients. Some were still experiencing the struggles and sting of a relationship that collapsed under the weight of distress. Despite their own wounds, each participant continues to be committed to walking with others as they misstep and falter in the journey of life, humans supporting each other from a place of vulnerability in order to connect, understand, and thrive.

As a therapist trained in Emotionally Focused Therapy, I am always in awe of clients who are willing to risk and go to those deep places, to be vulnerable with another human being despite previous battles and wounds. I sit with couples so committed to their relationship that they continue to reach even when standing on opposite sides of the Grand Canyon, knowing that they could tumble and land on the boulders below, knowing the excruciating pain of having your heart crushed. And, each time I facilitate training other therapists, I experience old wounds opening and at times find my eyes leaking as I mourn the loss of my own marriage. So, we all move forward, step by step, at our own pace, down diverse paths. For me, I am driven by my faith that God has a plan for me, and a hope that perhaps it will include being in a relationship that I can finally "get right."

REFERENCES

Abend, S. M. (1982). Serious illness in the analyst: Countertransference considerations. *Journal of the American Psychoanalytic Association, 30,* 365–379. doi:10.1177/000306518203000203

Acock, A. C., & Demo, D. H. (1994). *Family diversity and well-being.* Thousand Oaks, CA: Sage Publications.

Ahola, P., Valkonen-Korhonen, M., Tolmunen, T., Joensuu, M., Lehto, S. M., Saarinen, P. I., & Lehtonen, J. (2011). The patient–therapist interaction and the recognition of affects during the process of psychodynamic psychotherapy for depression. *American Journal of Psychotherapy, 65*(4), 355–379.

Ahrons, C. (1994). *The good divorce.* New York: Harper Collins.

Al-Mateen, C. S. (1991). Simultaneous pregnancy in the therapist and the patient. *American Journal of Psychotherapy, 45*(3), 432.

Anderson, T., Ogles, B. M., Pattersen, C. L., Lambert, M. J., & Vermeersch, D. A. (2009). Therapist effects: Facilitative interpersonal skills as a predictor of therapist success. *Journal of Clinical Psychology, 65,* 755–768. doi:10.1002/jclp.20583

Anker, M. G., Owen, J., Duncan, B. L., & Sparks, J. A. (2010). The alliance in couple therapy: Partner influence, early change, and alliance patterns in a naturalistic sample. *Journal of Consulting and Clinical Psychology, 78*(5), 635–645. doi:10.1037/a0020051

Aponte, H. J., & Carlsen, J. C. (2009). An instrument for person-of-the-therapist supervision. *Journal of Marital and Family Therapy, 35,* 395–405.

Aponte, H. J., & Kissil, K. (2014). 'If I can grapple with this I can truly be of use in the therapy room': Using the therapist's own emotional struggles to facilitate effective therapy. *Journal of Marital and Family Therapy, 40*(2), 152–164. doi:10.1111/jmft.12011

Aubuchon-Endsley, N. L., Callahan, J. L., & Scott, S. (2014). Role expectancies, race, and treatment outcome in rural mental health. *American Journal of Psychotherapy, 68*(3), 339–354.

Baldwin, M. (Ed.). (2000). *The use of self in therapy* (2nd ed.). New York: Hawthorne.

Baldwin, S., Wampold, B., & Imel, Z. (2007). Untangling the alliance–outcome correlation: Exploring the relative importance of therapist and patient variability in the alliance. *Journal of Consulting and Clinical Psychology, 75*(6), 842–852.

Bartle-Haring, S., Shannon, S., Bowers, D., & Holowacz, E. (2016). Therapist differentiation and couple clients' perceptions of therapeutic alliance. *Journal of Marital and Family Therapy, 42*(4), 716–730. doi:10.1111/jmft.12157

Basescu, C. (2009). Shifting ground: The therapist's divorce and its impact on her life and work. *Contemporary Psychoanalysis, 45*(1), 44–64.

Bass, A. (2007). When the frame doesn't fit the picture. *Psychoanalytic Dialogues, 17*(1), 1–27.

Baucom, B. R., Atkins, D. C., Rowe, L. S., Doss, B. D., & Christensen, A. (2015). Prediction of treatment response at 5-year follow-up in a randomized clinical trial of behaviorally based couple therapies. *Journal of Consulting and Clinical Psychology, 83*(1), 103–114. doi:10.1037/a0038005

Baucom, D. H., & Hoffman, J. A. (1986). The effectiveness of marital therapy: Current status and application to the clinical setting. In N. S. Jacobson & A. S. Gurman (Eds.), *Clinical handbook of marital therapy* (pp. 597–620). New York: Guilford Press.

Beckerman, N., & Sarracco, M. (2002). Intervening with couples in relationship conflict: Integrating emotionally focused couple therapy and attachment theory. *Family Therapy, 29*(1), 23–32.

Benish, S. G., Imel, Z. E., & Wampold, B. E. (2008). The relative efficacy of bona fide psychotherapies for treating post-traumatic stress disorder: A meta-analysis of direct comparisons. *Clinical Psychological Review, 28*, 746–758.

Berry, K., Gregg, L., Hartwell, R., Haddock, G., Fitzsimmons, M., & Barrowclough, C. (2015). Therapist–client relationships in a psychological therapy trial for psychosis and substance misuse. *Drug and Alcohol Dependence, 152*, 170–176.

Blatt, S. J., Sanislow, C. I., Zuroff, D. C., & Pilkonis, P. A. (1996). Characteristics of effective therapists: Further analyses of data from the national institute of mental health treatment of depression collaborative research program. *Journal of Consulting and Clinical Psychology, 64*(6), 1276–1284. doi:10.1037/0022-006X.64.6.1276

Blow, A. J., Sprenkle, D. H., & Davis, S. D. (2007). Is who delivers the treatment more important than the treatment itself? The role of the therapist in common factors. *Journal of Marital and Family Therapy, 33*, 298–317. doi:10.1111/j.1752-0606.2007.00029.x

Bohart, A. C., Elliott, R., Greenberg, L. S., & Watson, J. C. (2002). Empathy. In J. C. Norcross (Ed.), *Psychotherapy relationships that work: Therapist contributions and responsiveness to clients* (pp. 89–108). New York, NY: Oxford University Press.

Booth, A., & Amato, P. (1991). Divorce and psychological stress. *Journal of Health and Social Behavior, 32*, 396–407. doi:10.2307/2137106

Bray, J. H., & Jouriles, E. N. (1995). Treatment of marital conflict and prevention of divorce. *Journal of Marital and Family Therapy, 21*, 461–473.

Broderick, C. B., & Schrader, S. S. (1991). The history of professional marriage and family therapy. In A. S. Gurman & D. P. Kniskern (Eds.), *Handbook of family therapy* (Vol. 2, pp. 3–40). New York: Brunner/Mazel.

Brown, P. D., & O'Leary, K. D. (2000). Therapeutic alliance: Predicting continuance and success in-group treatment for spouse abuse. *Journal of Consulting and Clinical Psychology, 68*, 340–345.

Busby, D. M., & Holman, T. B. (2009). Perceived match or mismatch on the Gottman conflict styles: Associations with relationship outcome variables. *Family Process, 48*(4), 531–545.

Butler, M., Rodriguez, M., Roper, S., & Feinauer, L. (2010). Infidelity secrets in couple therapy: Therapists' views on the collision of competing ethics around relationship-relevant secrets. *Sexual Addiction and Compulsivity, 17*(2), 82–105, 24p. doi:10.1080/10720161003772041

Byrne, M., Carr, A., & Clark, M. (2004). The efficacy of behavioral couples therapy and emotionally focused therapy for couple distress. *Contemporary Family Therapy: An International Journal, 26*(4), 361–387.

Castonguay, L. G., & Beutler, L. E. (2006). Principles of therapeutic change: A task force on participants, relationships, and technique factors. *Journal of Clinical Psychology, 62*(1), 631–638.

Cheon, H., & Murphy, M. J. (2007). The self-of-the-therapist awakened. *Journal of Feminist Family Therapy, 19*, 1–16.

Christensen, A., Atkins, D. C., Baucom, B., & Yi, J. (2010). Marital status and satisfaction five years following a randomized clinical trial comparing traditional versus integrative behavioral couple therapy. *Journal of Consulting and Clinical Psychology, 78*(2), 225–235. doi:10.1037/a0018132

Clemente-Crain, V. A. (1996, June). Divorce and psychotherapy: The perceived impact of therapists' family of origin experience of divorce upon their practice of psychotherapy. *Dissertation Abstracts International, 56*, 7040.

Cookerly, J. R. (1980). Does marital therapy do any lasting good? *Journal of Marital and Family Therapy, 6*, 393–397.

Counselman, E. F., & Alonso, A. (1993). The ill therapist: Therapists' reactions to personal illness and its impact on psychotherapy. *American Journal of Psychotherapy, 47*(4), 591. ISSN: 00029564.

Crucible. In *Merriam-Webster.com*. Retrieved January 16th, 2017, from www.merriam-webster.com/dictionary/crucible

Deutsch, C. J. (1985). A survey of therapist's personal problems and treatment. *Professional Psychology: Research and Practice, 16*(2), 305–315. doi:10.1037/0735-7028.16.2.305

Doss, B. D., Cicila, L. N., Georgia, E. J., Roddy, M. K., Nowlan, K. M., Benson, L. A., & Christensen, A. (2016). A randomized controlled trial of the web-based our relationship program: Effects on relationship and individual functioning. *Journal of Consulting and Clinical Psychology, 84*(4), 285–296. doi:10.1037/ccp0000063

Efron, D., & Bradley, B. (2007). Emotionally focused therapy (EFT) and emotionally focused family therapy (EFFT): A challenge/opportunity for systemic and post-systemic therapists. *Journal of Systemic Therapies, 26*(4), 1–4. doi:10.1521/jsyt.2007.26.4.1

Emery, R. E. (1994). *Renegotiating family relationships: Divorce, child custody, and mediation*. New York: Guilford Press.

Evans, K., Kincade, E., & Seem, S. (2011). Ethics and values in feminist counseling and psychotherapy. In K. Evans, E. Kincade & S. Seem (Eds.), *Introduction to feminist therapy: Strategies for social and individual change* (pp. 25–56). Thousand Oaks, CA: Sage Publications.

Fletcher, S. E. (2015). *Cultural sensibility in healthcare: A personal & professional guidebook*. Indianapolis: Sigma Theta Tau International.

Friedlander, M. L., Lambert, J. E., Valentín, E., & Cragun, C. (2008). How do therapists enhance family alliances? Sequential analyses of therapist-client behavior in two contrasting cases. *Psychotherapy: Theory, Research, Practice, Training, 45*(1), 75–87. doi:10.1037/0033-3204.45.1.75

Fuertes, J. N., Gelso, C. J., Owen, J. J., & Cheng, D. (2013). Real relationship, working alliance, transference/countertransference and outcome in time-limited counseling and psychotherapy. *Counseling Psychology Quarterly, 26*(3/4), 294–312.

Garroutte, E. M., Sarkisian, N., Goldberg, J., Buchwald, D., & Beals, J. (2008). Perceptions of medical interactions between healthcare providers and American Indian older adults. *Social Science & Medicine, 67*(4), 546–556. doi:10.1016/j.socscimed.2008.04.015

Gellhaus Thomas, S. E., Werner-Wilson, R. J., & Murphy, M. J. (2005). Influence of therapist and client behaviors on therapy alliance. *Contemporary Family Therapy: An International Journal, 27*(1), 19–35.

Gelso, C. J. (2011). *The real relationship in psychotherapy: The hidden foundation of change*. Washington, DC: American Psychological Association.

References

Gelso, C. J., & Hayes, J. A. (2002). The management of countertransference. In J. C. Norcross (Ed.), *Psychotherapy relationships that work* (pp. 267–283). New York, NY: Erlbaum.

Gelso, C. J., & Hayes, J. A. (2007). *Countertransference and the therapists' inner experience: Perils and possibilities*. Mahwah, NJ: Erlbaum.

Gerson, B. (1996). *The therapist as a person: Life crises, life choices, life experiences, and their effects on treatment*. Hillsdale, NJ: Analytic Press, Inc.

Givelber, F., & Simon, B. (1981). A death in the life of a therapist and its impact on the therapy. *Psychiatry: Journal for the Study of Interpersonal Processes, 44*(2), 141–149.

Gladding, S. T. (2000). *Counseling: A comprehensive profession*. Upper Saddle River, NJ: Merrill.

Glass, C. R., Arnkoff, D. B., & Shapiro, S. J. (2001). Expectations and preferences. *Psychotherapy: Theory, Research, Practice, Training, 38*(4), 455–461. doi:10.1037/0033-3204.38.4.455

Gottman, J. M., & Gottman, J. S. (1999). The marriage survival kit: A research-based marital therapy. In R. Berger & M. T. Hannah (Eds.), *Preventive approaches in couples therapy*. Philadelphia, PA: Brunner/Mazel.

Gottman, J. M., & Krokoff, L. J. (1989). Marital interaction and satisfaction: A longitudinal view. *Journal of Consulting and Clinical Psychology, 57*, 47–52.

Greenberg, L. S., & Johnson, S. M. (1986). Affect in marital therapy. *Journal of Marital and Family Therapy, 12*, 1–10.

Greenman, P., & Johnson, S. (2013). Process research on EFT for couples: Linking theory to practice. *Family Process, Special Issue on Couple Therapy, 52*(1), 46–61.

Greenspan, M. (1984). Should therapists be personal? Self-disclosure and the therapeutic distance in feminist therapy. In D. Howard (Ed.), *The dynamics of feminist therapy* (pp. 5–17). New York: Hayworth Press.

Grunebaum, H. (1993). The vulnerable therapist: On being ill or injured. In J. H. Gold & J. C. Nemiah (Eds.), *Beyond transference* (pp. 21–50). Washington: American Psychiatric Press.

Gurman, A. S., & Fraenkel, P. (2002). The history of couple therapy: A millennial review. *Family Process, 41*(2), 199.

Guy, J. D., & Souder, J. K. (1986). Impact of therapists' illness or accident on psychotherapeutic practice: Review and discussion. *Professional Psychology: Research and Practice, 17*(6), 509–513. doi:10.1037/0735-7028.17.6.509

Hadžiahmetović, N., Alispahić, S., Tuce, Đ., & Hasanbegović-Anić, E. (2016). Therapist's interpersonal style and therapy benefit as the determinants of personality self-reports in clients. *Vojnosanitetski Pregled: Military Medical & Pharmaceutical Journal of Serbia, 73*(2), 135–145. doi:10.2298/VSP140911141H

Hafen Jr., M., & Crane, D. R. (2003). When marital interaction and intervention researchers arrive at different points of view. *Journal of Family Therapy, 25*(1), 4–14.

Hardin, S. I., & Yanico, B. J. (1983). Counselor gender, type of problem, and expectations about counseling. *Journal of Counseling Psychology, 30*, 294–297.

Håvås, E., Svartberg, M., & Ulvenes, P. (2015). Attuning to the unspoken: The relationship between therapist nonverbal attunement and attachment security in adult psychotherapy. *Psychoanalytic Psychology, 32*(2), 235–254. doi:10.1037/a0038517

Hayes, J. A., Gelso, C. J., Hummel, A. M. (2011). Managing countertransference. *Psychotherapy Theory Research Practice Training, 48*(1), 88–97. doi:10.1037/a0022182

Holliman, R., Muro, L., & Luquet, W. (2016). Common factors between couples therapists and imago relationship therapy: A survey of shared beliefs, values, and intervention strategies. *The Family Journal, 24*(3), 230–238. doi:10.1177/1066480716648693

Hull, C. L. (1944). Joseph Jastrow: 1863-1944. *The American Journal of Psychology, 57*, 581–585.

Ivey, A. E., D'Andrea, M., Ivey, M. B., & Simek-Morgan, L. (2007). *Theories of counseling and psychotherapy: A multicultural perspective.* Boston: Allyn & Bacon.

Jacobson, N. S., & Addis, M. E. (1993). Research on couples and couples therapy: What do we know? Where are we going? *Journal of Consulting and Clinical Psychology, 61*, 85–93.

Jacobson, N. S., Christensen, A., Prince, S. E., Cordova, J., & Eldridge, K. (2000). Integrative behavioral couple therapy: An acceptance-based, promising new treatment for couple discord. *Journal of Consulting and Clinical Psychology, 68*(2), 351–355. doi:10.1037/0022-006X.68.2.351

Johansen, K. H. (1993). Countertransference and divorce of the therapist. In J. H. Gold & J. C. Nemiah (Eds.), *Beyond transference* (pp. 87–108). Washington: American Psychiatric Press.

Johnson, N. J., Backlund, E., Sorlie, P. D., & Loveless, C. A. (2000). Marital status and mortality: The national longitudinal mortality study. *Annals of Epidemiology, 10*, 224–238. doi:10.1016/S1047-2797(99)00052-6

Johnson, S. M. (2007). A new era for couple therapy: Theory, research, and practice in concert. *Journal of Systemic Therapies, 26*(4), 5–16.

Johnson, S. M., & Talitman, E. (1997). Predictors of success in emotionally focused marital therapy. *Journal of Marital and Family Therapy, 23*, 135–152.

Joyce, A. S., Ogrodniczuk, J. S., Piper, W. E., & McCallum, M. (2003). The alliance as mediator of expectancy effects in short-term individual therapy. *Journal of Consulting and Clinical Psychology, 71*(4), 672–679. doi:10.1037/0022-006X.71.4.672

REFERENCES

Kalter, N., & Rembar, J. (1981). The significance of a child's age at the time of parental divorce. *American Journal of Orthopsychiatry, 51*(1), 85–100. doi:10.1111/j.1939-0025.1981.tb01351.x

Karson, M. (2008). *Deadly therapy: Lessons in liveliness from theater and performance theory.* Lanham, MD: Jason Aronson.

Karson, M., & Fox, J. (2010). Common skills that underlie the common factors of successful psychotherapy. *American Journal of Psychotherapy, 64*(3), 269–281.

Kiecolt-Glaser, J. K., & Newton, T. L. (2001). Marriage and health: His and hers. *Psychological Bulletin, 127*, 472–503. doi:10.1037/0033-2909.127.4.472

Kilgour, E., Kosny, A., McKenzie, D., & Collie, A. (2015). Healing or harming? Healthcare provider interactions with injured workers and insurers in workers' compensation systems. *Journal of Occupational Rehabilitation, 25*(1), 220–239. doi:10.1007/s10926-014-9521-x

Kim, D. H., Wampold, B. E., & Bolt, D. M. (2006). Therapist effects psychotherapy. *Psychotherapy Research, 16*, 161–172. doi:10.1080/10503300500264911

Kitchener, K. S., & Anderson, S. K. (2011). *Foundations of ethical practice, research, and teaching in psychology and counseling* (2nd ed.). New York, NY: Routledge.

Kitson, G. C. (1992). *Portrait of divorce: Adjustment to marital breakdown.* New York: Guilford Press.

Kocet, M. M., & Herlihy, B. J. (2014). Addressing value-based conflicts within the counseling relationship: A decision-making model. *Journal of Counseling and Development, 92*(2), 180–186.

Koenig, H. G. (Ed.). (1998). *Handbook of religion and mental health.* San Diego: Academic Press.

Kooperman, D. (2013). When the therapist is in crisis: Personal and professional implications for small community psychotherapy practices. *American Journal of Psychotherapy, 67*(4), 385–403.

Krumrei, E., Coit, C., Martin, S., Fogo, W., & Mahoney, A. (2007). Post-divorce adjustment and social relationships: A meta-analytic review. *Journal of Divorce and Remarriage, 46*(3/4), 145–166. doi:10.1300/J087v46n03_09

Lambert, M. J., Bergin, A. E., & Garfield, S. L. (2004). Introduction and historical overview. In M. J. Lambert (Ed.), *Bergin and Garfield's handbook of psychotherapy and behavior change* (pp. 3–15). New York, NY: John Wiley & Sons.

Lebow, J., Chambers, A., Christensen, A., & Johnson, S. (2012). Research of the treatment of couple distress. *Journal of Marital and Family Therapy, 38*(1), 145–168. doi:10.1111/j.1752-0606.2011.00249.x

Levengood, J., Ottaviano, K., & Chambliss, C. (1996). Relationship between therapists' knowledge about divorce effects and marital therapy intervention preferences. *Resources in Education*, ERIC/CAS. Retrieved from https://eric.ed.gov/?id=ED415477

Mamodhoussen, S., Wright, J., Tremblay, N., & Poitras-Wright, H. (2005). Impact of marital and psychological distress on therapeutic alliance in couples undergoing couple therapy. *Journal of Marital and Family Therapy*, *31*(2), 159–169. doi:10.1111/j.1752-0606.2005.tb01553.x

Markussen, S., Røed, K., Røgeberg, O. J., & Gaure, S. (2011). The anatomy of absenteeism. *Journal of Health Economics*, *30*, 277–292. doi:10.1016/j.jhealeco.2010.12.003

Marmarosh, C. L., Gelso, C. J., Markin, R. D., Majors, R., Mallery, C., & Choi, J. (2009). The real relationship in psychotherapy: Relationships to adult attachment, working alliance, negative transference, and therapy outcome. *Journal of Counseling Psychology*, *56*, 337–350. doi:10.1037/a0015169

Marshall, C., & Rossman, G. B. (2011). *Designing qualitative research* (5th ed.). Los Angeles, CA: Sage Publications.

Martin, D. J., Garske, J. P., & Davis, K. M. (2000). Relation of the therapeutic alliance with outcome and other variables: A meta-analytic review. *Journal of Consulting and Clinical Psychology*, *68*, 438–450.

Martin, P. (2011). Celebrating the wounded healer. *Counseling Psychology Review*, *26*(1), 10–19.

Martinez, J. S., Smith, T. B., & Barlow, S. H. (2007). Spiritual interventions in psychotherapy: Evaluations by highly religious clients. *Journal of Clinical Psychology*, *63*(10), 943–960.

Mathews, B. (1988, October). The role of therapist self-disclosure in psychotherapy: A survey of therapists. *American Journal of Psychotherapy*, *42*(4), 521. ISSN: 00029564.

McDowell, T., & Shelton, D. (2002). Valuing ideas of social justice in MFT curricula. *Contemporary Family Therapy*, *2*, 313–331.

Miller, G., & Baldwin, D. (2013). The implications of the wounded healer archetype for the use of self in psychotherapy. In M. Baldwin (Ed.), *The use of self in therapy*. Hove: Routledge.

Minuchin, S., Rosman, B., & Baker, L. (1978). *Psychosomatic families*. Cambridge, MA: Harvard University Press.

Miovic, M., McCarthy, M., Badaracco, M. A., Greenberg, W., Fitzmaurice, G. M., & Peteet, J. R. (2006). Domains of discussion in psychotherapy: What do patients really want? *American Journal of Psychotherapy*, *60*(1), 71–86.

Montagno, M., Svatovic, M., & Levenson, H. (2011). Short-term and long-term effects of training in emotionally focused couple therapy: Professional and personal aspects. *Journal of Marital and Family Therapy*, *37*(4), 380–392. doi:10.1111/j.1752-0606.2011.00250.x

Morrison, A. L. (1990). Doing psychotherapy while living with a life-threatening illness. In H. S. Schwartz & A. L. Silver (Eds.), *Illness in the analyst* (pp. 227–250). Madison, CT: International Universities Press.

REFERENCES

Moustakas, C. (1990). *Heuristic research: Design, methodology, and applications.* Newbury Park, CA: Sage Publications.

Myers, J. E., & Truluck, M. (1998). Health beliefs, religious values, and the counseling process: A comparison of counselors and other mental health professionals. *Counseling & Values, 42*(2), 106.

Nelson, T. S., Heilbrun, G., & Figley, C. R. (1993). Basic family therapy skills, IV: Transgenerational theories of family therapy. *Journal of Marital and Family Therapy, 19*, 253–266.

Nicoll, W. G. (1993). Multiple systems counseling: An integration and extension of Adlerian and systems theories. *Individual Psychology: The Journal of Adlerian Theory, Research and Practice, 49*(2), 132.

Niño, A., Kissil, K., & Apolinar-Claudio, F. L. (2015). Perceived professional gains of master's level students following a person-of-the-therapist training program: A retrospective content analysis. *Journal of Marital and Family Therapy, 41*(2), 163–176. doi:10.1111/jmft.12051

Nissen-Lie, H. A., Havik, O. E., Høglend, P. A., Monsen, J. T., & Rønnestad, M. H. (2013). The contribution of the quality of therapists' personal lives to the development of the working alliance. *Journal of Counseling Psychology, 60*(4), 483–495, 13p. doi:10.1037/a0033643

Nissen-Lie, H. A., Havik, O. E., Høglend, P. A., Rønnestad, M. H., & Monsen, J. T. (2014). Patient and therapist perspectives on alliance development: Therapists' practice experiences as predictors. *Clinical Psychology and Psychotherapy.* 22(4), 317–327. Doi:10.1002/cpp.1891

Norcross, J. C., & Wampold, B. E. (2011). Evidence-based therapy relationships: Research conclusions and clinical practices. *Psychotherapy, 48*(1), 98–102.

Olmstead, S. B., Blick, R. W., & Mills, L. I. (2009). Helping couples work toward the forgiveness of marital infidelity: Therapists' perspectives. *American Journal of Family Therapy, 37*(1), 48–66.

Ostroff, B. D. (2012). How does a therapist's divorce adjustment affect his or her therapy work? *Dissertation Abstracts International, 74*, 3544453.

Pack-Brown, S. P., Thomas, T. L., & Seymour, J. M. (2008). Infusing professional ethics into counselor education programs: A multicultural/social justice perspective. *Journal of Counseling and Development, 86*(3), 296–302.

Pappas, P. (1989). Divorce and the psychotherapist. *American Journal of Psychotherapy, 43*(4), 506–517.

Parsons, T. (1951). *The social system.* New York: Free Press.

Patterson, C. L., Uhlin, B., & Anderson, T. (2008). Clients' pretreatment counseling expectations as predictors of the working alliance. *Journal of Counseling Psychology, 55*(4), 528–534. doi:10.1037/a0013289

Pope, K., & Vasquez, M. (2011). *Ethics in psychotherapy and counseling: A practical guide* (4th ed.). Hoboken, NJ: Wiley.

Post, B. C., Wade, N. G., & Cornish, M. A. (2014). Religion and spirituality in group counseling: Beliefs and preferences of university counseling center clients. *Group Dynamics: Theory, Research, and Practice, 18*(1), 53–68. doi:10.1037/a0034759

Proulx, C. M., Helms, H. M., & Buehler, C. (2007). Marital quality and personal well-being: A meta-analysis. *Journal of Marriage and Family, 69*, 576–593.

Radcliff-Brown, A. R. (1952). *Structure and function in primitive society*. London: Cohen & West.

Ramseyer., F, & Tschacher, W. (2011). Nonverbal synchrony in psychotherapy: Coordinated body movement reflects relationship quality and outcome. *Journal of Consulting and Clinical Psychology, 79*(3), 284–295. doi:10.1037/a0023419

Raylu, N., & Kaur, I. (2012). Factors that affect treatment expectations of outpatients with substance use problems. *International Journal of Mental Health and Addiction, 10*(6), 804–817. doi:10.1007/s11469-012-9377-2

Richards, P. S., & Bergin, A. E. (Eds.). (2000). *Handbook of psychotherapy and religious diversity*. Washington, DC: American Psychological Association.

Riessman, C. K. (1990). *Divorce talk: Women and men make sense of personal relationships*. New Brunswick, NJ: Rutgers University Press.

Rober, P. (2011). The therapist's experiencing in family therapy practice. *Journal of Family Therapy, 33*, 233–255.

Rogers, C. R. (1957). The necessary and sufficient conditions of therapeutic personality change. *Journal of Consulting Psychology, 21*(2), 95–103.

Rønnestad, M. H., & Skovholt, T. M. (2012). *The developing practitioner: Growth and stagnation of therapists and counselors*. New York, NY: Routledge.

Rose, E. M., Westefeld, J. S., & Ansely, T. N. (2001). Spiritual issues in counseling: Clients' beliefs and preferences. *Journal of Counseling Psychology, 48*(1), 61–71. doi:10.1037/0022-0167.48.1.61

Sabatelli, R. M., & Bartle-Haring, S. (2003). Family of origin experiences and patterns of adjustment within couples. *Journal of Marriage and Family, 65*, 159–169.

Safran, J. D., Muran, J. C., & Proskurov, B. (2008). Theory, technique, and process in psychodynamic psychotherapy. In A. R. Levy & J. S. Ablon (Eds.), *Handbook of evidence-based psychodynamic psychotherapy* (pp. 201–226). New York: Humana Press.

Sager, C. J. (1966). The development of marriage therapy: An historical review. *American Journal of Orthopsychiatry, 36*(3), 458–467.

Sanberk, İ., & Akbaş, T. (2015). Psychological counseling processes of prospective psychological counselors: An investigation of client-counselor interactions. *Kuram Ve Uygulamada Eğitim Bilimleri, 15*(4), 859–878.

References

Sanders, R. K., Swenson III, J. E., & Schneller, G. R. (2011). Beliefs and practices of Christian psychotherapists regarding non-sexual multiple relationships. *Journal of Psychology and Theology, 39*(4), 330–344.

Satir, V. (2000). The therapist's story. In M. Baldwin (Ed.), *The use of self in therapy* (pp. 17–29). New York: The Haworth Press.

Schlachet, P. J. (1996). When the therapist divorces. In B. Gerson (Ed.), *The therapist as a person* (pp. 141–157). Hillsdale, NJ: The Analytic Press.

Shafranske, E. P. (Ed.). (1996). *Religion and the clinical practice of psychology.* Washington, DC: American Psychological Association.

Shane, E. (2002). The transformative effects of separation and divorce on analytic treatment. *Psychoanalytic Inquiry, 22*, 580–598. doi:10.1080/07351692209349004

Sharma, S., & Fowler, J. C. (2016). When countertransference reactions go unexamined due to predetermined clinical tasks: How fear of love can keep us from listening. *Psychotherapy, 53*(3), 302–307. doi:10.1037/pst0000089

Shetty, G., Sanchez, J. A., Lancaster, J. M., Wilson, L. E., Quinn, G. P., & Schabath, M. B. (2016). Oncology healthcare providers' knowledge, attitudes, and practice behaviors regarding LGBT health. *Patient Education & Counseling, 99*(10), 1676–1684. doi:10.1016/j.pec.2016.05.004

Simon, G. M. (2012). The role of the therapist: What effective therapists do. *Journal of Marital and Family Therapy, 38*(1), 8–12.

Simon, J. (1988). Criteria for therapist self-disclosure. *American Journal of Psychotherapy, 42*(3), 404.

Skovholt, T. M., & Jennings, L. (2004). *Master therapists: Exploring expertise in therapy and counseling.* Boston, MA: Allyn & Bacon.

Skowron, E. A., & Dendy, A. K. (2004). Differentiation of self and attachment in adulthood: Relational correlates of effortful control. *Contemporary Family Therapy, 26*, 337–357. http://dx.doi.org/10.1023/B:COFT.0000037919.63750.9d

Snyder, D. K., Mangrum, L. F., & Wills, R. M. (1993). Predicting couples' response to marital therapy: A comparison of short- and long-term predictors. *Journal of Consulting and Clinical Psychology, 61*(1), 61–69. doi:10.1037/0022-006X.61.1.61

Snyder, D. K., Wills, R. M., & Grady-Fletcher, A. (1991). Long-term effectiveness of behavioral versus insight-oriented marital therapy: A 4-year follow-up study. *Journal of Consulting and Clinical Psychology, 59*(1), 138–141. doi:10.1037/0022-006X.59.1.138

Softas-Nall, B., Beadle, M., Newell, J., & Helm, H. M. (2008). Spousal disclosure of extramarital relationships: Attitudes of marriage and family therapists. *Family Journal, 16*(4), 328–337.

Stevens, C. L., Muran, J. C., Safran, J. D., Gorman, B. S., & Winston, A. (2007). Levels and patterns of the therapeutic alliance in brief psychotherapy. *American Journal of Psychotherapy, 61*(2), 109–129.

Stone, D. (2008). Healing: Exploring the circle of compassion in the helping relationship. *The Humanistic Psychologist, 36*, 45–51.

Swanson, L. B. (2004). Phenomenology of divorce for young men. *Dissertation Abstracts International, 65*, 3203.

Tambling, R. B., & Johnson, L. N. (2010). Client expectations about couple therapy. *American Journal of Family Therapy, 38*(4), 322–333.

Tambling, R. B., Wong, A. G., & Anderson, S. R. (2014). Expectations about couple therapy: A qualitative investigation. *American Journal of Family Therapy, 42*(1), 29–41.

Tinsley, H. E., Workman, K. R., & Kass, R. A. (1980). Factor analysis of the domain of client expectancies about counseling. *Journal of Counseling Psychology, 27*, 561–570.

Wade, N. G., Worthington, E. J., & Vogel, D. L. (2007). Effectiveness of religiously tailored interventions in Christian therapy. *Psychotherapy Research, 17*(1), 91–105. doi:10.1080/10503300500497388

Walker, D. F., Gorsuch, R. L., & Tan, S. (2005). Therapists' use of religious and spiritual interventions in Christian counseling: A preliminary report. *Counseling and Values, 49*(2), 107–119.

Wallerstein, J. S. (1990). Transference and countertransference in clinical intervention with divorcing families. *American Journal of Orthopsychiatry, 60*(3), 337–345. doi:10.1037/h0079193

Wampold, B. E. (2001). *The great psychotherapy debate.* New Jersey: Lawrence Erlbaum Associates, Inc., Publishers.

Wang, H., & Amato, P. R. (2000). Predictors of divorce adjustment: Stressors, resources, and definitions. *Journal of Marriage and the Family, 62*, 655–668. doi:10.1111/j.1741-3737.2000.00655.x

Werner, C. M., Altman, I., Oxley, D., & Haggard, L. (1987). People, place and time: A transactional analysis of neighborhood. In W. H. Jones & D. Perlman (Eds.), *Advances in personal relationships.* Greenwich, CT: JAL.

Wertheimer, M. (2011). *Brief history of psychology* (5th ed.). New York: Psychology Press.

Wetzler, S., Frame, L., & Litzinger, S. (2011). Marriage education for clinicians. *American Journal of Psychotherapy, 65*(4), 311–336.

Winters, S., Rogers, L., Edwards, E., Levengood, J., Otaviano, K., & Chamblis, C. (1995). Relationship between therapists' gender and attitudes toward divorce and marital therapy intervention preferences. *Resources in Education,* ERIC/CAS,195.

REFERENCES

Wosket, V. (1999). *The therapeutic use of self: Counseling practice, research and supervision*. London: Routledge.

Zuroff, D., & Blatt, S. (2006). The therapeutic relationship in the brief treatment of depression: Contributions to clinical improvement and enhanced adaptive capacities. *Journal of Consulting and Clinical Psychology*, *74*(1), 130–140.

INDEX

Ainsworth, Mary, 59
Akbas, T., 17, 18
alliance *see* therapeutic alliance(s)
American Counseling Association
  (ACA), 123–124
American Psychological Association, 3
Aponte, H. J., 19
attachment-based approach, 63–64,
  115, 121–124
attunement, 23

Beck, Aaron, 12
being present, 60, 78, 84–85, 119
beliefs and views, expansion in
  previously held, 7–8
bitterness, 35–36, 77
Bowen, Murray, 59
bracketing, 25–26

Carlsen, J. C., 19
Clemente-Crain, V. A., 21
clients: concerns over self-disclosure by
  therapists, 92–93; expectations and
  gender of, 27; goals for, 104, 105–106;
  having difficulty being present in
  sessions, 84–85; questioning the
  credibility of divorced therapists,
  83–84; relational framing by, 27–28;

religious beliefs of, 24–25, 94–95;
  role expectations for therapists of,
  22; transference by, 79–80; *see also*
  counseling; divorced persons
Cognitive Behavioral Therapy
  (CBT), 68
counseling: attachment-based
  approach in, 63–64, 115, 121–124;
  being present in, 60, 78, 84–85, 119;
  Cognitive Behavioral Therapy (CBT),
  68; couples, 13–14; Emotionally
  Focused Therapy (EFT), 14, 33, 68,
  126; history of, 11–14; process of,
  14–29; process of healing in, 120–121;
  as shared experience, 14; *see also*
  clients; divorced therapists
countertransference, 19, 26, 71–72
couples counseling, 13–14
credibility, 7, 81–89
crucible, 15

divorce adjustment period, 21
divorced persons: in high conflict
  divorces, 77–78; questions to ask
  in working on self-awareness and
  recovery, 57–58; transference by,
  79–80; trying to stay a family, 49;
  well-adjusted, 21; *see also* clients

141

divorced therapists, 31–32; anger and sadness in, 122–123; being present in the therapeutic process, 60, 78; blender of emotions in, 43–45; blocks in own stuff of, 73; calm and peace in, 70; changing feelings about relationships in, 114–115; with children, 105–111; countertransference in, 19, 26, 71–72; credibility and wisdom of, 7, 81–89; empathy in, 62; encouraging disconnection, 103–111; feeling devastated and liberated, 42–43; feelings of hopelessness in, 114; finding happiness in second marriages, 105, 119; having more human element in role as mental health therapist, 117–118, 126; healing of, 120–121; impact of good new relationships on work by, 116–117; impact of own "stuff" on work by, 71–80, 114, 117, 124–125; less painful divorces of, 39–40, 74; mindfulness and introspection in, 120; not able to take time off from counseling, 63; pain felt by, 40–42, 85–86, 89, 101; painful enlightenment in, 32–34, 69–70, 75, 103; putting happiness on the backside, 37–38; remaining friends with their exes, 34–35; self-awareness in (*see* self-awareness); self-disclosure by, 28, 91–101; self-doubt and bitterness in, 35–36, 77; similarities and differences among surveyed, **45**; special insights of, 117–123; still trying to detach, 36–37; taking time off from counseling, 66; triggers for, 72–73, 79; *see also* counseling; therapists
divorce statistics, 2–3

Ellis, Albert, 12
Emotionally Focused Therapy (EFT), 14, 33, 68, 126

empathy and understanding, 5, 62
enlightenment through divorce, 32–34, 103
ethical bracketing, 25–26
expansion in previously held views and beliefs, 7–8
exploration of self, 8–9

family of origin (FOO): acceptance of divorce in, 49–50; being supportive in divorce situations, 50, 55; influence of, 48; with negative views of divorce, 49–55; religious beliefs and, 48, 49–50; values on finding love and, 47
family values, 47
forced changes, 15
Fowler, J. C., 60
Freud, Sigmund, 12, 59, 71, 91

Gerson, B., 6
Gottman, John, 89
Grunebaum, H., 23

Hall, G. Stanley, 11
Hendricks, Harvel, 89
high-conflict divorces, 77–78
history of counseling, 11–14
human and vulnerable therapists, 9–10

introspection, 120

Jastrow, Joseph, 12
Johns Hopkins University, 11
Johnson, Sue, 14, 89

Levengood, J., 22
love, ways to find, 47

Maslow, Abraham, 12
mindfulness, 120
Motivational Interviewing (MI), 68

National Association of Social Workers, 3
Native American clients, 22
Nelson, 59

INDEX

older non-traditional students, 33
Ostroff, B. D., 16

painful enlightenment in divorce, 32–34, 69–70, 75, 103
parts of self, 57
person-of-the-therapist, 4, 8–9, 19–21, 24, 28–29, 31, 125; self-awareness and, 60, 66
Power of Now, The, 89
psychoanalysis, 12
Psychology Today, 14

Ramseyer, F., 23
recovery: in counseling, 120–121; self-care in, 119; value of self-awareness in, 58–59; *see also* self-awareness
relational framing, 27–28
relationship gurus, 114
religious beliefs, 24–25, 48, 49–50; credibility and wisdom of therapists and, 87; impacted by divorce, 55–56, 122; self-awareness and, 67–68; self-disclosure and, 94–95
research on divorced therapists, 3–5
Rogers, Carl, 12
role expectations of therapists, 22

Sanberk, I., 17, 18
Satir, Virginia, 59
secular therapists, 24–25
self-awareness, 8–9, 119; attachment-based approach in, 63–64; versus Band-Aid on problems, 62–63; calm and peace with, 70; as most valuable element in recovery, 58–59; necessary for effective counseling, 60; painful memories and, 69–70; personal counseling for, 64–69; person-of-the-therapist and, 60, 66; questions to ask in exploring, 57–58; religious beliefs and, 67–68; self-of-the-therapist and, 59; utilizing friends for, 67

self-care, 119
self-disclosure, 28; after clients ask, 100; clients' negative reactions to, 98–99; emotions brought up by, 93–94; as essential for therapeutic alliance, 91; reasons for, 93; therapists on client concerns over, 92–93; therapists that avoid, 94–96, 98–100; therapists' worries about client reactions to, 96–98; trickiness of, 91–92; when it is beneficial to the client, 99–100
self-doubt, 35–36
self-of-the-therapist, 15, 19, 113, 125; self-awareness and, 59
Shane, 27
shared experience, counseling as, 14
Sharma, S., 60
signature themes, 19
Skinner, B. F., 12
Solution Focused theory, 105–106

therapeutic alliance(s), 12, 17; collaboration and empathetic engagement in, 18–19; creation of, 5–6, 18; importance of self-disclosure in, 91; person-of-the-therapist and, 19–21
therapeutic presence, 119
therapists: bracketing by, 25–26; creating an alliance, 5–6; credibility or wisdom of, 7; empathy and understanding of, 5; expansion in previously held views and beliefs, 7–8; goals of, 1; as human and vulnerable, 9–10; impact of personal life crises experienced by, 21–24; moving forward in changing relationships, 113–126; older non-traditional students as, 33; research on, 3–5; returning to work after personal crisis, 23; role expectations of, 22; secular versus religious, 24–25; self-awareness of, 8–9; self-disclosure by, 28; trained to be "tabula rasa," 2; *see also* divorced therapists

143

transference, 79–80
trauma response, 18
triggers, emotional, 72–73, 79
Tschacher, W., 23

University of Leipzig, 11

vocational counseling, 12

Wallerstein, J. S., 26
well-adjusted divorced persons, 21
wisdom, 7, 81–89
Wundt, Wilhelm, 11